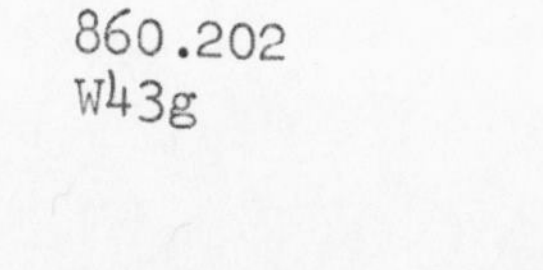

WITHDRAWN
L. R. COLLEGE LIBRARY

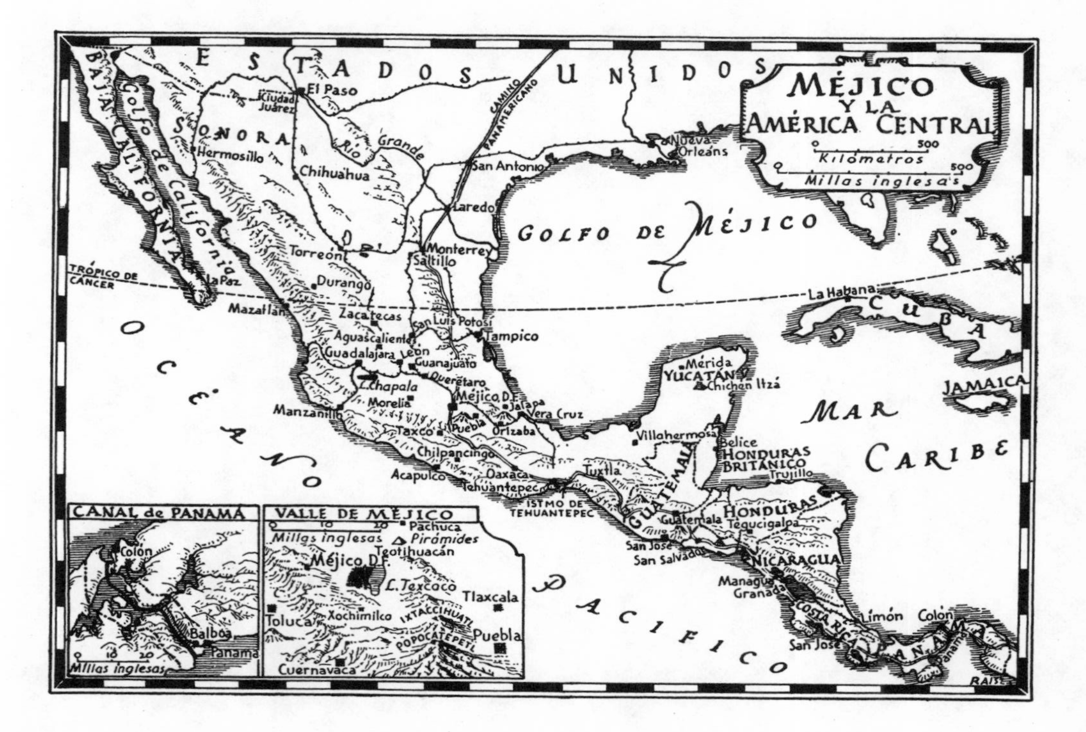
MÉJICO Y LA AMÉRICA CENTRAL
0 500
Kilómetros
0 500
Millas inglesas
ESTADOS UNIDOS
El Paso
Kiudad Juárez
SONORA
Hermosillo
Chihuahua
Río Grande
CAMINO PANAMERICANO
San Antonio
Nueva Orleans
Laredo
Monterrey
Saltillo
Torreón
BAJA CALIFORNIA
Golfo de California
La Paz
TRÓPICO DE CÁNCER
Durango
Mazatlan
Zacatecas
San Luis Potosí
Tampico
Aguascalientes
Guadalajara
León
Guanajuato
L. Chapala
Querétaro
Morelia
Méjico D.F.
Jalapa
Vera Cruz
Manzanillo
Taxco
Puebla
Orizaba
Chilpancingo
Acapulco
Oaxaca
Tehuantepec
ISTMO DE TEHUANTEPEC
GOLFO DE MÉJICO
La Habana
CUBA
JAMAICA
Mérida
YUCATÁN
Chichen Itzá
MAR CARIBE
Villahermosa
Belice
HONDURAS BRITÁNICO
Trujillo
Tuxtla
GUATEMALA
HONDURAS
Guatemala
Tegucigalpa
San José
San Salvador
NICARAGUA
Managua
Granada
COSTA RICA
Limón
Colón
San José
PANAMÁ
OCÉANO PACÍFICO
CANAL de PANAMÁ
Colón
Balboa
Panamá
0 10 20
Millas inglesas
VALLE DE MÉJICO
0 10 20
Millas inglesas
Pachuca
Pirámides
Teotihuacán
Méjico D.F.
L. Texcoco
Tlaxcala
Toluca
Xochimilco
IXTACCIHUATL
POPOCATEPETL
Puebla
Cuernavaca
RAISZ

A GUIDE TO STUDIES IN SPANISH AMERICAN LITERATURE

BY

NINA LEE WEISINGER

UNIVERSITY OF TEXAS

GREENWOOD PRESS, PUBLISHERS

WESTPORT, CONNECTICUT

The Library of Congress has catalogued this publication as follows:

Library of Congress Cataloging in Publication Data

Weisinger, Nina Lee, 1895-
A guide to studies in Spanish American literature.

Original ed. issued in series: Heath modern language series.
1. Spanish American literature--Outlines, syllabi, etc. I. Title.
PQ7081.W4 1972 860'.2'02 78-148646
ISBN 0-8371-6010-3

Originally published in 1940
by D. C. Heath and Company, Boston

Reprint by permission of D. C. Heath and Company

Reprinted from an original copy in the collections
of the University of Illinois

First Greenwood Reprinting 1972

Library of Congress Catalogue Card Number 78-148646

ISBN 0-8371-6010-3

Printed in the United States of America

FOREWORD

With the recent appearance in the field of Spanish American studies of a new anthology and the first part of a detailed treatise on the novel, material is now available for guidance in the study of all fields of Spanish American literature. The purpose of this outline survey *Guide*, which has developed in connection with classroom work, is to present the literary production of Spanish America according to movements and genres, with references to current manuals and anthologies for critical comment or for text. There seems to be a need for a manual of this nature to correlate the material at hand. It is hoped that the *Guide* will be of service not only to instructors and students in our institutions but also to persons outside of academic circles who may be interested in Spanish American literary life.

In view of the fact that the field of Spanish American literary production, especially in poetry, is remarkably wide, even the number of good poets being enormous, this *Guide* does not aim to be exhaustive; it strives, rather, to give an outline along broad lines of the several literary forms and movements that have manifested themselves from colonial times to the present. There is no fixed order in which the *Guide* is to be followed after the colonial and revolutionary epochs have been considered. The study of dramatic production, for instance, might precede the consideration of modernism, since interest in play writing dates, for practical reasons, from the early days immediately following the colonization of the New World.

The omission of brief resumés or suggestions as to content of many novels, poems, etc., is intentional: the compiler of the *Guide* wishes to encourage first-hand acquaintance with the works which are here placed in certain categories. If ready-made resumés are desired, they may often be found in the texts to which references are given. On the blank pages of the *Guide* the students may write their own summaries or reactions to the material read.

Because of the intimate relation of literary works to historical or political events in the New World, a reference chronology of Spanish American history is included in the *Guide*.

Grateful acknowledgment for criticism and suggestions for the improvement of the *Guide* is hereby made to Professor Americo Castro and to Professor J. R. Spell of the University of Texas.

N. L. W.

A GUIDE TO STUDIES IN SPANISH AMERICAN LITERATURE

With reference to the following works:

ALFRED COESTER: *The Literary History of Spanish America* (Macmillan, 2nd ed., 1928)

—— —— *Anthology of the Modernista Movement in Spanish America* (Ginn, 1924)

G. D. CRAIG: *The Modernist Trend in Spanish American Poetry* (University of California Press, 1934)

ISAAC GOLDBERG: *Studies in Spanish-American Literature* (Brentano's, 1920)

HILLS and MORLEY: *Modern Spanish Lyrics* (Holt, 1913)

H. A. HOLMES: *Spanish America in Song and Story* (Holt, 1932)

ROSENBERG and TEMPLIN: *A Brief Anthology of Mexican Prose*

—— —— —— *A Brief Anthology of Mexican Verse* (Stanford University Press, 1928)

JULIO JIMÉNEZ RUEDA: *Historia de la Literatura Mexicana* (Editorial "Cultura," Mexico, 1928)

E. SOLAR CORREA: *Poetas de Hispanoamérica* (Imp. Cervantes, Santiago de Chile, 1926)

ARTURO TORRES-RÍOSECO: *Antología de la Literatura Hispanoamericana* (Crofts, 1939)

—— —— *La Novela en la América Hispana* (University of California Press, 1939)

—— —— *Grandes Novelistas de América* (In press)

NINA LEE WEISINGER: *Spanish American Readings* (Heath, 1929)

The above works are cited as follows: Coes., *Lit. Hist.*, *Ant.;* Craig; Gold.; Hills-Mor.; Hol.; Ros.-Tem., *Prose*, *Verse;* Jim. R.; Solar; Tor., *Ant.*, *La nov.*, *G. N. de A.;* Weis.

CONTENTS

A GUIDE TO STUDIES IN SPANISH AMERICAN LITERATURE

A GUIDE TO STUDIES IN SPANISH AMERICAN LITERATURE

COLONIAL PERIOD (1500–1800)

While the literary production of this period belongs to Spanish letters, and an account of its principal writers and their works is included in the histories of Spanish literature, it must also be taken as the beginning of the literary life of the New World. A monument like *La Araucana*, the work of a young Spaniard whose stay in Peru and Chile was brief but who participated actively in the military campaigns of that period, is considered a masterpiece of Chilean poetry. As was natural, the earlier works were written by Spaniards who were on American soil more or less temporarily; but gradually American-born authors rose to prominence, and toward the close of the colonial epoch allegiance to Spain had become so weak that many literary men were American in spirit.

A. Historical Works. During the years of discovery, exploration, and conquest, historical writing flourished, in both prose and poetry, but of the numerous productions only a few deserve mention, along with their authors.

1. Hernando Cortés (1485–1547). Of all the *Cartas de relación* written by the *conquistadores* to their Spanish monarchs, those of Cortés to Charles V are the most important. There are five of them, written during 1522–1524, concerning his conquest of Mexico (1519–1521) and related matters. English translations of these *cartas* are available.
2. Alvaro Núñez Cabeza de Vaca (1490?–1559?). In *Naufragios* (1542) he describes his own explorations and adventures in the territory which now forms our Gulf states.
3. Fray Bartolomé de las Casas (1474–1566). The "Apostle of human liberty," so called because of his

tireless efforts to defend the Indians from exploitation by the Spanish conquerors. Of his several works the most significant are *Historia general de las Indias* (written 1552–1561, published 1875), which describes the explorations of 1492–1520 (he came over with Columbus), and *Destrucción de las Indias* (1552), which deals with the inhuman treatment that was meted out to the indigenes. He became Bishop of Chiapas, in Mexico.

4. The Inca Garcilaso de la Vega (1540–1616). Son of a companion of Pizarro and an Inca princess, he was peculiarly fitted to write of the Peruvian Indians before the conquest and of the wars that followed the arrival of the Spanish invaders. The first South American writer of importance. His masterpiece is *Los comentarios reales de los incas del Perú* (Part I, 1609; Part II, 1616), which gives a vivid and realistic account of the Inca empire and of its conquest by the Spaniards, as well as of the civil strife which followed the conquest.
5. Alonso de Ercilla y Zúñiga (1533–1594). His masterpiece, the best Golden Age epic of Spanish literature, is *La Araucana,* based on his personal adventures during the insurrection of the Araucanian Indians of Chile against the invading Spaniards (three parts, published 1569, 1578, 1590). The first work of real merit composed in the Americas; written and published before the *Comentarios reales* of Garcilaso de la Vega, but dealing with subsequent events.
6. Pedro de Oña (16th cent.) Born in Chile and its foremost poet during the colonial epoch. His *Arauco domado* (1596), covering the same events as *La Araucana,* was written to extol the exploits of Don García Hurtado de Mendoza, governor of Chile, whom Ercilla, for personal reasons, had slighted in his poem. A long religious poem, *El Ignacio de Loyola* (1636) in honor of that saint, added greatly to Oña's fame.

B. Poets. The title of foremost poet of colonial times belongs to Ercilla y Zúñiga, whose *La Araucana* is, by virtue

of its subject matter, classed with the leading historical works of the period. Of the hundreds of lesser lights who wrote innumerable verses few won sufficient renown to survive the oblivion their work merited.

1. Bernardo de Balbuena (1568–1627). Author of the second best epic of Spain's Golden Age, *El Bernardo o la Victoria de Roncesvalles* (1624), he was the first poet of America. His most important poem, *La grandeza mexicana* (1604), describes vividly the wealth of natural beauties and abundance of mineral resources of Mexico. In later life Balbuena was Bishop of Puerto Rico.
2. Carlos de Sigüenza y Góngora (1645–1700). Mexican. A mathematician, scientist, and scholar whose poetic output suffered from the tedious conceits of Gongorism. His best remembered poem celebrates the legend of Our Lady of Guadalupe, patron saint of Mexico.
3. Sor Juana Inés de la Cruz (1651–1695). " La Décima Musa Mexicana." A brilliant woman and the first feminist of America, whose fame in learning and literature filled all New Spain, although she spent her life after seventeen as a nun in a convent. In recent years there has been a revival of interest in her and in the three volumes of her collected works (first vol. published 1689), in which are found, besides her poems, some religious plays and her two comedies (the second written in collaboration). Her best-known verses, and the only ones widely read today, are the satirical *Redondillas* in which she scores the detractors of women.

C. Drama. See A, Colonial Drama, pp. 50–54.

1. Juan Ruiz de Alarcón (1581?–1639)
2. Fernán González de Eslava (16th cent.)
3. *Ollantay* (between 1770 and 1780)
4. Manuel José de Labardén (1754–1809)

Coes., *Lit. Hist.*, pp. 1–28; Bardin, *El reino de los incas;* Weis., pp. 27–54; Ros.-Tem., *Prose*, pp. xiii–xviii, 3–7; Ros.-Tem., *Verse*, pp. xiv–xvi, 5–12; Hol., pp. 141–143, 348, 430; Tor., *Ant.*, pp. 139–145

REVOLUTIONARY EPOCH (1800–1825)

I. *In South America*

A. Historical Background. What may be truly called Spanish American literary production begins with this period and, since it was a literature of occasion, some knowledge of the events of the struggle for independence is indispensable for the comprehension of it.

1. Causes of the Revolution. The generative, or cumulative, causes were principally the economic and political restrictions imposed upon the colonies by Spain and the examples of successful revolutions by the North American colonists and in France. The immediate, or precipitating, causes of open rebellion were the seizure of Buenos Aires by the English (1806, 1807) and the invasion of Spain by Napoleon (1808–1814), the latter giving rise to the establishment of "juntas" in America which later became centers for fomenting patriotism and hostilities.
2. Outstanding Military Leaders. Two revolutions, waged simultaneously and independently under the leadership of their respective military geniuses, united their victorious forces in Peru for the final defeat of Spain's power in South America.
   (*a*) In the south, after Manuel Belgrano's preliminary achievements in Argentina (1812, 1813), José de San Martín successfully prosecuted the war, passing from his training camp at Mendoza (1814–1817) to victories in Chile at Chacabuco (1817) and Maipú (1818), dislodging the Spanish troops from Lima (1821), and leaving the completion of the conquest to triumphant Bolívar (1822).
   (*b*) With equal success in the north, Bolívar, taking command after the defeat of Miranda, had liberated Colombia, Venezuela, and Ecuador (victorious at Boyacá in 1819, at Carabobo in 1821, and at Quito in 1822), and after the withdrawal of San Martín he vanquished the remaining Spanish forces

in brilliant victories at Junín, August, 1824, and at Ayacucho, December, 1824.

Coes., *Lit. Hist.*, pp. 39–44, 52–55, 61–63

B. Literary Production. During the progress of military activities men of talent were aiding the struggle with pen and sword, inspired by current events and in turn inspiring patriotic effort in their countrymen.

1. Mariano Moreno (1778–1811). First secretary of the junta of Buenos Aires, director of *La Gaceta de Buenos Aires*, founder of the national library and of a school of mathematics.
2. Vicente López y Planes (1784–1856). Argentine soldier-poet, captain of the famous company of "Los Patricios," and author of the *Marcha patriótica* which at once became and is now the national hymn of Argentina.
3. Gregorio Funes (1749–1829). Dean of the cathedral of Córdova. Argentine historian, writing chiefly for military purposes his three volume *Ensayo de la historia civil de Buenos Aires, Tucumán y Paraguay.*
4. Camilo Henríquez (1769–1825). Priest, poet, soldier of Chile. Member of "La Sociedad del Buen Gusto" of Buenos Aires, for which he wrote, as a vehicle to express his ideas on education and religion, a play entitled *Camila o la patriota de Sud América.*
5. Esteban de Luca (1786–1824). Argentine poet of merit, mathematician, metallurgist, artillery sergeant, manager of a cannon foundry.
6. Bartolomé Hidalgo (1787–?). Precursor of the Argentine writers of gaucho verse. Best known for his ironical dialogues of *Chano y Contreras* concerning conditions in and around Buenos Aires resulting from the revolution.

Coes., *Lit. Hist.*, pp. 43–52, 57–61; Hol., 453–455

C. The Master Poets. While the masterpieces of two great neoclassicists were published subsequent to the final vic-

tories of the revolution, their inspiration is wholly of this period.

1. José Joaquín Olmedo (1780–1847), the "singer of Junín," author of some thirty compositions, owes his fame chiefly to two heroic odes: *La victoria de Junín* (1825), written to glorify Bolívar, and *Al general Flores, vencedor en Miñarica* (1835), superior in some respects to the former ode. Greek and Roman classic influence is very pronounced in Olmedo's work. The poet was active as a political leader and occupied various posts of honor and influence in Peru and Ecuador.
2. Andrés Bello (1781–1865), a native of Venezuela but more definitely identified with the intellectual and civic life of Chile, was a profound scholar, a masterful educator, and a prolific writer. As poet his finest expression is in his *Silva a la agricultura de la zona tórrida* (1826). Menéndez y Pelayo calls Bello "a consummate master of poetic diction, learnedly picturesque, laboriously polished."

Coes., *Lit. Hist.*, pp. 64–69, 72–78; Hol., 329–332, 502–506; Hills-Mor., pp. 193–198, 214–220; Solar, pp. 17–31

II. *In North America*

Two centers of revolution existed also in North America.

A. Mexico. The same economic and political restrictions on the part of the Spanish colonial government which provoked discontent and, finally, open rebellion in South America produced similar results in Mexico, though the course of hostilities was different.

1. First Revolution. In September of 1810 a rebellion began in the province of Guanajuato under the leadership of a rural priest, Father Miguel Hidalgo, and Ignacio Allende. Early in 1811 these two leaders were captured and executed. José María Morelos continued the struggle until his capture and execution in 1815, after which the insurrection was gradually put down.
2. Second Revolution. In 1820 the privileged classes, led

by Augustín Iturbide, opened a new rebellion, and the following year the last viceroy signed the Treaty of Cordova in recognition of the independence of Mexico.

Coes., *Lit. Hist.*, pp. 79–83

3. Literary Production

(*a*) Poetry. Political events of the period were not inspired by ardent, patriotic poems of occasion, as was the case in South America. But these events were the inspiration of poetic expression that came after the success of the revolution. Then vigorous odes to the heroes appeared: *A Hidalgo* and *Al suplicio de Morelos*, by Wenceslao Alpuche (1804–1841); *Al 16 de septiembre de 1821*, by Quintana Roo (1787–1851); *El Grito de Independencia*, by Ochoa y Acuña (1783–1833); *A Iturbide en su coronación*, by Francisco Ortega (1793–1849). A fine poem in honor of Morelos is *Romance heroico de la salida de Morelos de Cuautla*, by Sánchez de Tagle (1782–1847).

(*b*) Prose. The revolution had a champion among the intellectuals whose fearless expressions, published for the most part as pamphlets by "El Pensador Mexicano," cost him imprisonment. The place in Mexican letters, however, of José Joaquín Fernández de Lizardi (1774–1827) is due chiefly to a picaresque novel, *El Periquillo Sarniento* (1816), a satirical picture of the conditions in Mexico at that time. He wrote other novels of less merit. As Mexico's first outstanding journalist he wielded great influence by his political articles and his novels, and his work is indispensable today for the study of the conditions of the epoch.

Coes., *Lit. Hist.*, pp. 84–89; Hol., 393–395; Ros.-Tem., *Prose*, xx–xxii, 23–28

B. Cuba. The only revolutionary center which did not emerge from the struggle with independence in the first quarter of the century. This refuge for loyalists and hotbed of

conspiracies produced Cuba's greatest poet, José María Heredia (1803–1839). For his participation in a revolt young Heredia was banished for life. His deeply subjective poetry reflects the sadness and nostalgia, and at times melancholy, induced in his spirit by his banishment. Most noteworthy among his poems are his ardent odes addressed to various manifestations of nature.

Coes., *Lit. Hist.*, pp. 89–103; Hol., pp. 262–265; Tor., *Ant.*, pp. 148–152; Hills-Mor., pp. 179–190; Solar, pp. 32–37

ROMANTICISM (1832–1888)

During the period of political agitation following the close of the revolutionary era European romanticism entered the literary world of most of the newborn republics-to-be. Many of the romanticists were prominent figures in political affairs, and, as in the turbulent days of Rosas' dictatorship in Argentina, were frequently forced to flee for their lives to foreign refuge.

A. Argentine Romanticists. Particularly in this republic was the soil propitious for the growth of the new movement, and numerous poets, a large proportion of them followers of the gaucho school, made contributions of more or less merit.

1. Esteban Echeverría (1805–1851). Returning from five years of study in France, including a visit to England, thoroughly converted to romanticism, he introduced the new movement by the publication (1832) of a long poem of little merit entitled *Elvira o la novia del Plata.* In his masterpiece, *La cautiva* (1837), he practised with marked success his doctrine for the Americanization of poetry:

   > La poesía entre nosotros . . . preciso es . . . que, reflejando los colores de la naturaleza física que nos rodea, sea a la vez el cuadro vivo de nuestras costumbres y la expresión más elevada de nuestras ideas dominantes, de los sentimientos y pasiones que nacen del choque inmediato de nuestros sociales intereses . . .

His influence and that of his theory of aesthetics prevailed during a great part of the 19th century. So great was Byron's influence upon Echeverría that he has been often called " the Argentine Byron." Active in politics and bitterly hostile to Rosas, Echeverría founded a secret society, " La Asociación de Mayo " (1837), to combat the Federalist party and bring about the downfall of the tyrant.

2. José Mármol (1817–1871). Poet, dramatist, novelist, the memory of him today rests largely on his novel *Amalia* (1852), written to expose the evils and tragic degradation caused by the tyranny of Rosas, whom he hated violently. His poems are held in esteem for their lyrical beauty or for their sincerity and intensity of feeling.
3. Bartolomé Mitre (1821–1906). Soldier, poet, president, historian, to whom Argentina is greatly indebted for his services to the nation after the fall of Rosas (1852). His romanticism is at its best in his *Rimas* (1854), many of which were written in his earlier years. He gave the first poetic treatment of Santos Vega, the legendary troubadour of the Pampa; when the use of gaucho verse became popular among later poets, he raised his voice in protest against the use of the gaucho's jargon, maintaining that poetry should give a poetic interpretation of nature and primitive customs. After leaving the presidency of Argentina in 1868, he founded *La Nación*, still a leading Argentine daily, and wrote, among other historical works, his monumental *Historia de San Martín* (1888).
4. Juan María Gutiérrez (1809–1878). A man of broad scholarship and prolific pen; a disciple of Echeverría in both political and literary ideals and a member of the Asociación de Mayo, his chief romantic work is the long poem *Los amores del payador*, marked by the author's usual fine diction, refinement, and good taste. In later life Gutiérrez was for many years rector of the University of Buenos Aires.
5. Domingo Faustino Sarmiento (1811–1888). A brilliant

journalist, politician, educator, diplomat, president, reformer predominantly interested in the cause of popular education, a man of many talents and boundless energy. In his study of educational systems, he traveled in Europe and the United States, imbibing new ideas which he brought home and put into practice. Although his writings comprise fifty volumes, he owes his literary fame chiefly to his widely known *Facundo o la civilización y la barbarie* (1845), an illuminating book for the student of Argentine history which presents a detailed study of the gaucho and his influence on social life and government.

6. Hilario Ascasubi (1807–1875). Another enemy of Rosas who barely escaped with his life. Like Mitre he collected and used legends about Santos Vega, the mythical minstrel of the Pampa, but unlike Mitre he gave a " faithful reproduction of nature " by using the gaucho's jargon in his verse. His best-known work today is his long poem, a sort of picaresque novel in verse, on *Santos Vega o los mellizos de la Flor* (1872), first published in 1851 as dramatic sketches of the life and character of the gaucho.
7. Estanislao del Campo (1834–1880). Also among the poets who employed the idiom of the gaucho, he is now remembered only for his clever and delightful *Fausto* (1866), a popular long poem giving the impressions and reactions of a well-known gaucho who had attended a performance of the opera *Faust* in the old Colón theater of Buenos Aires. Act by act the poet retells with delicate artistry the story of *Faust*, filling it with gaucho sentiment and homely realism.
8. José Hernández (1834–1886). Author of the masterpiece of the gaucho school, *Martín Fierro* (1872) with its sequel, *La vuelta de Martín Fierro* (1878). Both poems have enjoyed an immense popularity ever since their publication; they give a minute portrayal of gaucho traditions, habits of thought, and philosophy of life; while highly romantic in tone and interspersed with passages of beautiful lyric quality, they contain

many touches of realism in instances of official blundering or injustice toward the untutored children of the Pampa. The language of the poems is the picturesque vernacular condemned by Mitre. Like the legend concerning the death of Santos Vega and the inner meaning of the subtitle of *Facundo* (*La civilización y la barbarie*), the work of Hernández symbolizes the fruitless struggle of the primitive gaucho against the advance of European immigration and progress.

9. Rafael Obligado (1851–1920). A worthy disciple of Echeverría and Mitre, he consummated in his verses the deification of Santos Vega. His first poems on this theme, the three composing his *Tradiciones argentinas* (1845), comply with Mitre's demand for poetical interpretation, and the last edition of his poems (1906) contains *El himno de Santos Vega*, for which the author has been greatly praised and called "the national poet par excellence." As a man of wealth, Obligado wrote for pleasure; as a lover of the Greek and Roman classics, he had deep regard for beauty of language and form; and as an ardent patriot with genuine feeling for nature, he chose his subjects from native sources. An interesting episode of his literary life was his debate in verse with Calixto Oyuela on the respective merits of classicism and romanticism.
10. Eduardo Gutiérrez (1853–1890). One of the first to put the gaucho into prose. His character by the name of Juan Moreira, hero of the novel of this title, became almost as well known as Martín Fierro, though he degenerated into a notorious criminal. Gutiérrez also opened the door for the entrance of the gaucho into the theater by dramatizing an episode of his *Juan Moreira* for a circus pantomime. From this small beginning there arose a type of *criollo* plays, and the gaucho found a permanent place in national drama.
11. Olegario Víctor Andrade (1841–1882). Considered by some critics the greatest of all Argentine poets. Because of poverty his education was limited and superficial, a defect which is not overshadowed by the grandilo-

quence of much of his work. His verses are most effective when read aloud; as Menéndez y Pelayo says, "Escribió para ser leído en voz alta y resonante, y para ser aplaudido a cañonazos." His most popular poem is *El nido de cóndores* (1877), written to reproach the people of Argentina for not having brought home the remains of San Martín (died in France in 1850). The intense Americanism of Andrade insures him a place of esteem among American, if not Spanish, readers.

Coes., *Lit. Hist.*, pp. 106–157; Weis., pp. 55–112; Hol., pp. 11–40; Tor., *Ant.*, pp. 158–164; Hills-Mor., pp. 151–161; Solar, pp. 57–60, 79–82, 86–89

B. Romanticism in Other Countries. The movement touched the literary life of each of the newly liberated, struggling nations, but with varying degrees of intensity, making only a ripple in some fields, and inspiring few writers of works of merit in others.

1. In Uruguay. Next to Argentina, her sister nation across the river Plate produced the most important romanticists, of whom two are outstanding.

(*a*) Alejandro Magariños Cervantes (1825–1893). A versatile, dominating literary figure and rector of the University of Montevideo, his greatest fame rests upon his *Celiar*, a poetic gaucho legend (1852). His best novel in prose, *Caramurú*, also deals with a gaucho hero, and pictures in detail gaucho life and customs.

(*b*) Juan Zorrilla de San Martín (1857–1931). Uruguay's greatest poet and one of the great poets of South America. His masterpice, *Tabaré* (1888), called the masterpiece of Uruguayan literature, is typically American and is concerned with the relations between the Charrúas, native Indians of Uruguay, and the early Spanish colonists. The long narrative poem has a simple plot which unfolds in a series of beautiful, melodious lyrics.

Coes., *Lit. Hist.*, pp. 172, 176–179, 182–184; Hol., pp. 453–457; Solar, pp. 100–105

2. In Chile. Here romanticism, brought by expatriates fleeing from Rosas, met with opposition from the disciples of Andrés Bello. But one of Bello's sons, Carlos, wrote a romantic play, *Los amores del poeta* (1842), which was received with much acclaim, and Juan Bello likewise accepted the new manner and wrote in it. Neither of these, however, rose to the place attained by two other Chileans of their generation.

   (*a*) Salvador Sanfuentes (1817–1860). A distinguished pupil of Andrés Bello who rose to prominence in political life and became a Supreme Court Judge. Best known for his poetic legends and a romantic drama, *Juana de Nápoles* (1850). He was the most prolific of all Chilean poets and always displayed genuine feeling for nature.

   (*b*) Guillermo Blest Gana (1829–1904). While he wrote dramas and prose tales, he is best remembered for his verses, particularly his sonnets, in all of which he is often deeply subjective. Like Sanfuentes he wrote poetic legends, but he is not a poet of nature. Love and death were among his favorite themes. *Versos* (1854), *Armonías* (1884), and *Sonetos y fragmentos* (1907) are his chief poetic works.

Coes., *Lit. Hist.*, pp. 197–206, 211, 212; Hol., pp. 143–145; Solar, pp. 67–72

3. In Peru. Probably because the Peruvian temperament is gay and fun-loving, romanticism here gave the world no poet of eminence. Of the goodly number who followed the fashion of the day the most notable was Carlos Augusto Salaverry (1831–1890). The melancholy expressed in his verses is genuine, the product of the misfortunes and woes of his personal life. A beautiful love elegy entitled *¡ Acuérdate de mí !* is his most widely appreciated poem.

Coes., *Lit. Hist.*, pp. 248–250; Hol., pp. 410–412; Solar, pp. 73, 74

4. In Bolivia. Of scanty white population and for many years a victim of political turmoil, Bolivia's literary production has been meager. Its half dozen romanticists are of slight importance in the intellectual life of the continent.

Coes., *Lit. Hist.*, pp. 262, 263; Hol., pp. 97–101

5. In Ecuador. The country which claims as its own one of the outstanding poets of the new world, Olmedo, also takes pride in a most versatile writer who, later in the same century, attained excellence in both verse and prose and was acclaimed beyond the Atlantic: Juan León Mera (1832–1899). In many of his poems and in his best-known novel, *Cumandá* (1879), Mera expresses his love for the Indian traditions. *La virgen del Sol*, a long poetic legend, has won much applause, and *Cumandá* led the Spanish critic Valera to rank its author with Cooper and Chateaubriand.

Coes., *Lit. Hist.*, pp. 270, 271; Hol., pp. 332–336; Solar, 75–78

6. In Colombia. In this nation's galaxy of literary men the romanticists shine brightly. Surrounded by natural scenery of staggering beauty and variety, and blessed with a rich historical heritage, it was easy for the poets of the romantic generation to be borne aloft on the wings of inspiration and wield a strong influence which is still felt in Colombia.

   (*a*) José Joaquín Ortiz (1814–1892). The classical finish of his romantic poems somewhat overshadows their inspiration. Less prolific than some of his contemporaries, he has left several compositions of decided merit; for example, *Los colonos*, which Menéndez y Pelayo praised as one of the finest jewels of American poetry, descriptive and lyrical at the same time.

   (*b*) José Eusebio Caro (1817–1853). Close friend and

co-editor of Ortiz, who published his poems. Prominent in the political life of Bolívar's republic of Nueva Granada, Caro wrote ardent political verse as well as vigorous romantic lyrics, many of which record events of his life. One of his most worthy compositions is his spirited, sympathetic poem entitled *En boca del último inca.*

(*c*) Julio Arboleda (1817–1862). Though rich and educated in London, he was a staunch patriot and rose to the rank of colonel in the army. His later political activities cost him many inconveniences, loss of property, and finally his life. Of his poetic works the best is *Gonzalo de Oyón*, a romantic epic poem based upon legend, whose interest involves the relations of early Spanish conquistadores with the Indians.

(*d*) Gregorio Gutiérrez González (1826–1872). The most popular Colombian poet. His pen name of "Antioco" was known to everybody, and even servants knew his verses by heart. The evident sincerity in the expression of his sentiments and in the descriptions of his beloved province of Antioquía endeared him to all classes of readers. His longest and most famous poem is didactic, *Memoria sobre el cultivo del maíz en Antioquia.*

(*e*) Jorge Isaacs (1837–1895). Though he was a romantic poet of no mean ability, the widespread fame of Isaacs rests upon his idyllic prose-poem *María* (1867), which has been translated into many languages. Of simple plot and action, this novel gives fine character portrayal against a background of exquisite natural scenery in the Cauca valley of Colombia.

Coes., *Lit. Hist.*, pp. 275–288, 300–302; Hol., pp. 213–220, 242; Hills-Mor., pp. 162–167; Solar, pp. 61–66

7. In Venezuela. Nature is usually the inspiration of the Venezuelan romanticists, and lyrical sweetness a characteristic of their verse.

(*a*) José Antonio Maitín (1804–1874). The leading representative of romanticism in his country was inspired by the luxuriance of nature in the valley of the Choroní where he lived in peace on his estate. His best-known poem is the *Canto fúnebre* which he wrote in memory of his wife.

(*b*) José Ramón Yepes (1822–1881). A naval officer of distinction and a fine poet of nature known familiarly as " the Swan of the Lake." His pictorial and descriptive talents were exceptional, and his themes, as well as the lyrical quality of his verses, are reminiscent of Shelley.

(*c*) José Antonio Calcaño (1827–1897). He loved to imitate various French, Italian, English, and Spanish romanticists, and his compositions cover a wide range of emotions and poetic forms. A delicate feeling for landscape is one of his conspicuous traits.

(*d*) Domingo Ramón Hernández (1829–1893). A tender, melancholy poet greatly beloved by his fellow countrymen. His gentle philosophy of life is nowhere more exquisitely expressed than in the little poem which pictures a child gathering butterfly wings: *Alas de mariposas.*

Coes., *Lit. Hist.*, pp. 308–314; Hol., pp. 507–512; Solar, pp. 49–52

8. In Mexico. The melancholy strain which is indigenous in all Mexican literature, because it is innate in the Mexican temperament, together with an unsurpassed heritage of legends and history, offered a fertile field for the flourishing of romanticism.

(*a*) Ignacio Rodríguez Galván (1816–1842). The leader of romanticism in Mexico. As the nephew and clerk of a bookseller in the capital, he had early access to romantic poems and dramas imported from Europe. In 1838 he produced *Muñoz, Visitador de México,* the first romantic drama to appear in this country. But his masterpiece is *La profecía de Guatemoc,* a poetic legend concerning the Aztecs.

The Aztec theme also appears in another of his poetic legends, *La visión de Moctezuma.*

(*b*) Fernando Calderón y Beltrán (1809–1845). Ranked among Mexico's best poets, he owes most of his fame to his eight popular dramas, of which the most important are *Ana Bolena, El torneo,* and the comedy *A ninguna de las tres.* In imitation of Espronceda's pirate song he wrote *El soldado de la libertad.* An example of his best lyrics is his tender *A una rosa marchita.*

(*c*) Manuel María Flores (1840–1885). Reputed to have been the most widely read Mexican poet of his day, he is best known for his volume of *Pasionarias,* whose title suggests the sensual nature of his verse, in which kisses and caresses abound to satiety. Though a brilliant poet in his day, he died poor, blind, and all but forgotten by his contemporaries.

(*d*) Manuel Acuña (1849–1873). A brilliant poet who fell a victim to the materialistic doctrines of science and died a suicide at the age of twenty-four. He is best represented by two widely different poems: *Ante un cadáver,* an expression of his belief in materialism; and *Nocturno a Rosario,* an anguished outpouring of love to a young woman who had rejected his wooings.

Coes., *Lit. Hist.,* pp. 335–339, 348, 350; Weis, pp. 155–167; Hol., pp. 349–353, 357–360, 369, 370; Hills-Mor., pp. 200–206; Tor., *Ant.,* pp. 153–157; Ros.-Tem., *Verse,* pp. 22–26, 42–46

9. In Cuba. The passion for liberty which characterized Cuba's literary production until the end of the nineteenth century is outstanding in its contribution to romanticism.

(*a*) "Plácido" — Gabriel de la Concepción Valdés (1809–1844). A quadroon born in the humblest circumstances, brought up by his paternal grandmother, who was a negro ex-slave, he possessed a genuine poetic gift which raised him to such a

prominent place among Cuban singers of liberty that he fell a victim to the suspicion of the Spanish authorities and was shot, though vigorously protesting his innocence, on a charge of participation in a political conspiracy. In addition to his beautiful nature lyrics, he is accredited with the exquisite *Plegaria a Dios* which became known after his execution.

(*b*) José Jacinto Milanés y Fuentes (1814–1863). Beautiful tropical local color forms the setting of his poems, most of which were written in the seven-year period preceding the twenty years of mental trouble which clouded his life. His verses were, and continue to be, popular because of their description of Cuban life, their mild melancholy, and their moral qualities.

(*c*) Juan Clemente Zenea (1832–1871). Another poet and patriot shot by the Spaniards because he expressed, perhaps too impetuously, his yearning for liberty. Some of his elegiac poems reveal great perfection of form. A tender melancholy and a subjective note pervade much of his verse.

(*d*) Gertrudis Gómez de Avellaneda (1814–1873). Although most of her literary output was published in Spain (where she spent nearly all her life) and belongs to Spanish literature, Spanish America claims her with great pride as its greatest woman writer. Some of her best poems owe their inspiration to her love for her native Cuba. She wrote in both the classic and the romantic schools, her models in the latter being Lamartine and Byron. Feeling rather than depth of thought characterizes her poems, since love, both human and divine, was the impelling force of her life as well as of her pen.

Coes., *Lit. Hist.*, pp. 379–381, 405, 406, 409–413; Weis., pp. 113–128; Hol., pp. 265–269; Hills-Mor., pp. 190–192

10. In Puerto Rico. Culturally this island belongs to Spanish America, its literary activity dating from co-

lonial times when Bernardo de Balbuena was bishop there. (See p. 6, B, 1.) One of its best poets, if not the best, is José Gautier Benítez (1848–1880), author of a celebrated poem entitled *¡ Puerto Rico !* in which the island is addressed by its musical Indian name of Borinquen. This beautiful poem of 229 verses is reminiscent of Bello's famous *Silva* addressed to the torrid zone.

Coes., *Lit. Hist.*, p. 439; Hol., p. 309

THE "MODERNISTA" MOVEMENT (1888–1910)

As romanticism waned there developed a new school of poets, with an intermingling of prose writers, most of whom were greatly influenced by the French Parnassians and symbolists. The publication of Rubén Darío's *Azul* in 1888 marked the definite launching of the movement.

A. The Precursors. Among the writers who manifested the new tendencies and methods which Darío welded into a clearly defined poetic style, four men of different nationality were outstanding.

1. Manuel Gutiérrez Nájera (1859–1895). Rated among Mexico's best poets of all time, *el Duque Job* possessed a delicate soul full of music which reveled in the melodious verses of his French models. His great contribution to the new movement was the introduction of the musical quality of French into Spanish verse and prose. After him, it has been said, there is more music in verse, and prose is lighter and more luminous, enlivened with beautiful new figures and images. Among his highly successful musical compositions are *La serenata de Schubert* and a masterpiece of verbal sound, *A la Corregidora.* In his prose and many of his poems we find a delicate humor and a marked degree of the melancholy characteristic of the Mexicans, both of these qualities being prominent in his *Cuentos color de humo y cuentos frágiles.* Nearly all of his work is deeply subjective.

2. Julián del Casal (1863–1893). Neurasthenic and tubercular, the poetic work of his brief, unhappy life reflects the constant, unwholesome introspection of which he was a victim. His psychology is clearly expressed in *Nostalgias*, a poem truly *modernista* in its form and its exotic elements. Casal contributed some new metrical forms and revived others of earlier periods. Baudelaire was his chief model.
3. José Asunción Silva (1865–1896). Possessing physical beauty, an aristocratic spirit, and rare culture, this gifted, tortured soul was driven to the brink of madness by his misfortunes and his unceasing self-analysis. Baudelaire, Verlaine, and Poe influenced him profoundly. His metrical innovations, of which *Nocturno* (*III*) is a widely known example, the inward musical quality of his verse, his endless questioning of life and the enigma of existence, his utter pessimism and spiritual darkness, and his "infinite horror of death" are striking characteristics of *modernista* poetry. On a Sunday morning in May he gave up his struggle with fate and ended his life with a pistol. His tomb is in the Strangers' Cemetery outside his native Bogotá.
4. José Martí (1853–1895). Wholly different from the other precursors in life and spirit was Martí, whom Torres-Ríoseco aptly calls "grande en todo." This apostle of Cuban independence loved life and action, simplicity and sincerity, liberty and happiness for himself and all human kind. His political activities for the freedom of Cuba took him to many lands, and resulted in his death in an encounter on Cuban soil with a detachment of Spanish soldiers. In his two volumes of poetry, *Ismaelillo* (tender verses about his son) and *Versos sencillos* (love lyrics), as well as in his abundant prose, he expressed himself as a rule with clarity and technical perfection. His fine prose style had a direct influence upon Darío, whom all modernists recognized as the master of the new school.

Coes., *Lit. Hist.*, pp. 363–365, 450–457; Coes., *Ant.*, pp. 6–56; Hol., pp. 364–367, 284, 285, 228, 229, 278–283; Weis., pp.

180–198; Tor., *Ant.*, pp. 165–175; Gold., pp. 1–64; Tor., *Precursores del modernismo*

B. The Outstanding "Modernista" Writers

1. The Leader: Rubén Darío (1867–1916). A native of the small republic of Nicaragua, his genius lifted him above territorial boundaries and made him a native of all Spanish America. Different nations at one time or another named him as their diplomatic representative to foreign powers, and he resided in or visited several countries besides Nicaragua. Prolific in both prose and verse, he has been rated as the greatest Spanish-speaking poet of the last hundred years. The musical quality of his prose and verse, his metrical innovations, and the broad range of his inspiration are among the notable features of his production. He loved wealth, but lived in poverty. Often a bitter cynicism is manifest in his work because he felt that the poet, as well as other artists, is not appreciated in this materially minded world.

   The stages of Darío's poetic growth may be noted in his best volumes of verse, which appeared at irregular intervals: *Azul* (1888), impressionistic stories and poems of his maturing youth revealing his desire for the ideal; *Prosas profanas* (1896), in which he is the best exponent of modernism, loving the rare and unusual, the exquisite and the sumptuous, and expressing his artistic ideals with great metrical freedom and in new poetic forms; *Cantos de vida y esperanza* (1905), containing forceful poems of racial and international importance and some of Darío's most melodious and best-known lyrics; *El canto errante* (1907), in which the poet has become a universal character depicting the beauty which he beholds everywhere in his wanderings.

   Even more prolific in prose than in verse, Darío's numerous volumes of criticism, travel, etc., appeared from 1885 until his death, and several more were published posthumously.

Coes., *Lit. Hist.*, pp. 458–466, *Ant.*, pp. 57–136; Hol., pp. 119–128; Tor., *Ant.*, pp. 175–180; Goldberg, pp. 101–183; Hills-Mor., pp. 211–213; Solar, pp. 148–161; Torres, *Rubén Darío*, 1931, Harvard University Press

2. Other Eminent *Modernista* Writers. As in the case of romanticism, this movement had its followers in practically every Spanish American nation, most of them being poets, though prose also had good representatives. But comparatively few modernists rank sufficiently high to be considered among the outstanding literary men of the continent or of their respective countries.

(*a*) Amado Nervo (1870–1919). Standing next to Darío is a prolific Mexican who enjoyed prestige in Spain as well as throughout Hispanic America. He spent much of his life in diplomatic service, dying while minister to Uruguay. His funeral procession to Vera Cruz on an Argentine battleship, accompanied by cruisers of other nations, has been called the greatest event of the century in the New World. All Latin America was represented at his funeral in Mexico City. A master of prose as well as of verse, Nervo's complete works comprise twenty-nine volumes.

Coes., *Lit. Hist.*, p. 469, *Ant.*, pp. 211–230; Hol., pp. 371–375; Tor., *Ant.*, pp. 182, 183; Solar, pp. 171–177; Gold., pp. 75–81; Weis., pp. 199–214

(*b*) José Santos Chocano (1875–1934). Peruvian. Often called " the poet of America " because of his fondness for New World themes, which is seen especially in his most popular volume, *Alma América* (1906). Hotheaded and prone to adventure, his not always worthy episodes ended with his assassination in Chile. His energetic spirit is expressed in one of his widely known mottoes: " O encuentro camino o me lo abro ! "

Coes., *Lit. Hist.*, pp. 469–471, *Ant.*, pp. 179–207; Hol., pp.

415–417; Tor., *Ant.*, pp. 188–190; Solar, pp. 196–201; Gold., pp. 246–293

(*c*) José Enrique Rodó (1872–1917). The greatest prose writer of the school and one of Uruguay's leading men of letters. His masterpiece, *Ariel* (1900), an essay addressed to Spanish American youth, has had considerable influence upon the thinking of the southern continent. Rodó is generally conceded to be the best literary critic of his epoch, and he stands supreme in the field of the philosophical essay.

Coes., *Lit. Hist.*, pp. 470, 471, *Ant.*, pp. 148–159; Hol., pp. 484–488; Tor., *Ant.*, pp. 129–132; Gold., pp. 184–245

(*d*) Enrique González Martínez (1871–). Perhaps the best contemporary Mexican poet and a well-known diplomat. His impatience with certain phases of modernism found expression in a famous sonnet entitled *Tuércele el cuello al cisne* (in *Los senderos ocultos*, 1911). His spirit and message to the world are perhaps best expressed in the poem *Busca en todas las cosas* (also in *Los senderos ocultos*).

Coes., *Lit. Hist.*, p. 481, *Ant.*, pp. 208–210; Hol., p. 375; Tor., *Ant.*, p. 184; Gold., pp. 82–92; Solar, pp. 181–184

(*e*) Leopoldo Lugones (1874–1938). One of the most prominent of the literary associates of Darío during the latter's stay in Buenos Aires. A prolific writer of multiple talents, distinguished both for his prose and for his verse, and at home in the classic, romantic, or *modernista* manner. In his later poems he had made the transition from *modernista* to realistic verse. Aside from his abundant literary production Lugones rendered long service in the educational system of Argentina.

Coes., *Lit. Hist.*, pp. 468, 469, *Ant.*, pp. 142–147; Hol., 44–46; Tor., *Ant.*, p. 191; Solar, pp. 162–170

(*f*) Delmira Agustini (1890–1914). Born in Montevideo. She is outstanding among the five Spanish American women who have in recent years won recognition with their poetry (the other four are Alfonsina Storni, Argentina; Juana de Ibarbourou and Luisa Luisi, Uruguay; and Gabriela Mistral, Chile). By some critics Delmira Agustini is considered the greatest woman poet America has produced. The dominant note of the four volumes of verses written in her brief life reveals the vague but intense emotions of woman's soul at the altar of love.

Coes., *Lit. Hist.*, p. 482; Hol., p. 461; Tor., *Ant.*, p. 203; Solar, p. 217

CLASSIC POETRY

At the head of all Spanish American classicists stand Bello and Olmedo. But after them, in all periods, no matter what type of poetry was new or popular, there has been some cultivation of verse along classic lines, and conservative poets have never ceased to find favor. Often these poets practised the doctrine enunciated by Echeverría for the Americanization of literature. Years before Echeverría the celebrated ode of Labardén entitled *Al Paraná* anticipated the source of inspiration of many subsequent poets of varying schools. (See 2*c*, p. 54.) Of the numerous poets coming under this classification only the following need be mentioned here.

1. Francisco Acuña de Figueroa (1790–1862). A foe of independence in the revolutionary period, he later became so ardent a patriot that he wrote Uruguay's national hymn. But a foe of romanticism he remained to the end. His fame rests upon his twelve volumes of classic verses, one of his most effective poems being *La madre africana*, written in protest against Uruguay's participation in African slave trade.
2. Carlos Guido y Spano (1827–1918). An Argentine classicist with a sympathetic appreciation of his compatriot romanticists. To his reverence for correct form he added a love for the tender and sentimental, and this combination

made him a wise judge in the debate on classicism vs. romanticism submitted to him for decision by Obligado and Oyuela. His *Nenia* has been called "one of the most precious gems of Argentine lyrism."

3. Calixto Oyuela (1857–). A prize winner for his classic verses in the "Juegos florales" of Buenos Aires in the eighties and an uncompromising foe of romanticism. His *Eros* is a masterpiece of sentiment expressed in exquisite form.
4. Miguel Antonio Caro (1843–1909). Colombia's most eminent man of letters of his generation and oldest son of José Eusebio Caro of the romantic school. He founded the Colombian Academy of letters and served his republic as president. The classic ideal and finish of his poems are well marked. Among the best-known and most lauded is a short ode to Bolívar, *A la estatua del Libertador*, in which he stresses certain moral aspects of the Liberator's character. Caro loved the Greek and Latin classics, and his translation of Virgil is ranked as the best in Spanish.
5. Alejandro Tapia y Rivera (1827–1882). A talented and industrious writer of Puerto Rico who produced lyric and epic poetry, dramas, stories, and novels. In many respects his greatest work was his fantastic *La Sataniada* (1878), upon which he worked sixteen years and which he ranked as the finest of the world's great epics. Neither his contemporaries nor posterity agreed with him, although the very lengthy poem contains many admirable verses and passages.

Coes., *Lit. Hist.*, pp. 37, 38, 150–154, 169–171, 291, 440; Hol., pp. 6, 25, 42, 452, 226; Hills-Mor., pp. 171–174

DRAMATIC PRODUCTION

A. Colonial Drama. Although the history of the early drama in Spanish America is obscure, it is evident that from the beginning of the Spanish occupation of the New World interest was manifested in dramatic performances, both for religious instruction and for social entertainment. From the pen of one of the first twelve Franciscan missionaries who came to New Spain in 1524, Fray Toribio de Bena-

vente, we have a description of a rather elaborate *auto* picturing the fall of Adam and Eve and their expulsion from the Garden of Eden, a play performed in 1538 by the Indians in their own language. Later the intellectual and social life centering in the courts of the viceroys was enlivened by frequent theatrical functions, particularly upon the arrival of a new viceroy, the birth of a prince, or some other event of prime interest in the Old World or the New.

1. Religious Drama. Two types appear: plays intended for the conversion and instruction of the Indians, which were sometimes adaptations of native ceremonial dances or translation into the native tongues of Spanish plays and *autos* familiar in religious ceremonies; *loas* and allegorical pieces produced for the entertainment of the colonists and to celebrate some event of state. Among the former are the *Auto sacramental del Hijo Pródigo* by Juan de Espinosa Medrano, the anonymous *Usca Paucar*, and Calderón's *La Aurora en Copacabana.*
2. Secular Drama. In both New Spain and Peru plays were adapted to the Indian tongues or composed in them for the entertainment of the natives. A conspicuous example is *Ollantay*, a drama in the Quechua language in Peru whose authorship has long been a matter of dispute. Among the colonists the theater was soon thoroughly established. At first the plays presented were those of the mother country, Spanish in theme and authorship. Soon plays written by Spaniards on American subject matter became popular, such as *Hazañas de don García Hurtado de Mendoza, Los españoles en Chile,* and *Arauco Domado.* Later, as was natural, dramas by American-born authors upon American themes found a place in the theater. The first work of this type in Chile is said to have been *Hércules chileno* (Caupolicán), performed in Concepción in 1693 to celebrate the arrival of the Governor's bride. At about the same time the Franciscan Father Agustín de Vetancourt published his *Teatro mexicano.* A few dramatists are worthy of mention.

(a) Juan Ruiz de Alarcón (1581?–1639). Though he spent most of his life in Spain and belongs among the great dramatists of Spain's *Siglo de Oro*, some authorities believe that he learned the dramatic art in Mexico and that his native land may justly claim to have given him the outstanding characteristics of his art. Because two of his comedies contain numerous expressions peculiar to Mexico, some critics believe that they were composed there, especially since he was a graduate of the University of Mexico. His finest work, however, clearly belongs to Spain. Two of his best-known plays are *La verdad sospechosa*, showing the ill results of lying, and *Las paredes oyen*, which attacks slander.

(b) Fernán González de Eslava (16th cent.). Probably of Andalusian birth, he spent his life in Mexico. Best known for the sixteen allegorical plays in the collection entitled *Coloquios espirituales y sacramentales*, printed in 1610. One value of his work is the light it sheds upon the speech current in Mexico in his day.

(c) Manuel José de Labardén (1754–1809). A native of Argentina and educated in Peru, he has the honor of being the precursor of Argentine national dramatists. The scene of his *Siripo*, enacted in 1789 but read to friends years before, is the Pampa, its subject matter being the conflict between the early colonists and the aborigines. Of the three acts of the tragedy there survive only the second and one scene of another. It is hoped that a complete copy will come to light in some private library.

Coes., *Lit. Hist.*, pp. 29–33, 37, 38; Hol., pp. 439, 440

B. EVOLUTION OF THE LATER DRAMA. During the revolutionary era there was enthusiastic activity in the writing and performance of plays in Argentina, Colombia and other sections, but little of permanent worth was produced. Of the plays enacted in Buenos Aires or read before "La Sociedad del Buen Gusto," organized in 1817 for the purpose of promoting the drama, one of the most noteworthy is

Camila o la patriota de Sud América, written by Camilo Henríquez, a Chilean. Its present value lies in the information it contains concerning the ideas on education and religion held in that period. After the establishment of independence from Spain the course of development of the drama is perhaps best seen by a separate consideration of a few different countries.

1. In Argentina. Several well-marked types which appeared in the history of dramatic production led to the formation of a national theater.

   (*a*) Classic Drama: Juan Cruz Varela (1794–1839). *Dido* (1823) and *Argía* (1824), based on Latin and Greek models, were among the most original plays written for "La Sociedad del Buen Gusto" and were popular for their references to the troubled political situation in Argentina.

   (*b*) Romantic Drama: José Mármol (1817–1871). Of slight literary merit are *El poeta* (1842) and *El cruzado* (1851), plays in verse favorably received by the public, which deserve mention only for their place in the chronological development of the theater.

   (*c*) Gaucho Drama. Of considerable significance was the first appearance of the gaucho in the circus performances of the famous Podestá brothers, who adapted to melodramatic pantomime certain portions of *Juan Moreira*, the popular novel of Eduardo Gutiérrez. When, a few years later, dialogue was added to the performance, the seed was sown for the true national theater in Argentina. *Martín Fierro* and *Santos Vega* were also successfully staged by the Podestás, and then various playwrights tried their hand at original gaucho plays which met varying degrees of success on the stage. Thus originated a new genre which has never entirely left the theater.

   (*d*) National Drama: Martín Coronado (1840–1919). The Argentine theater is greatly indebted to Coronado for his contribution to its evolution and stabili-

zation. Between 1877 and 1917 he produced twenty-four plays (most of them after 1900) of such variety and merit that he furnished the theater with a cultured repertory sufficiently large to lift it out of the formative period and raise it to a height where the semi-barbaric creole theater was fused with the cultured European theater. Coronado's most famous play, *La piedra de escándalo,* first staged in 1902 by the Podestás, marked at the same time the height of his production and of the Argentine national theater. A run of 500 consecutive performances attests its popularity. A well-organized play of three acts and in verse, it observes the classic unities, but its emotional and musical qualities, the sensational types of character portrayed, and some of the situations presented make it a romantic play. The " piedra de escándalo " is the young daughter of a rural family who, after a tragic elopement with a city seducer who later deserts her, returns home to the great mortification of her older sister and brothers.

(*e*) Florencio Sánchez (1875–1910). Since 1900 a legion of playwrights have produced scores of plays which have reached the stage, but no dramatist or play has deserved undying fame. Among those who will perhaps be longest remembered, Florencio Sánchez is one who has found favor among American readers. Although a native of Uruguay, his years spent in Argentina and his dramatic production staged in Buenos Aires have identified him with the Argentine theater. Of his twenty plays performed between 1903 and 1909 the two most conspicuous for their national inspiration are *M'hijo el dotor* (1903) and *La Gringa* (1904). Both of these were complete successes and netted their author substantial financial returns.

(*f*) Pablo Groussac (1848–1929). A French boy who immigrated to Argentina grew up to become one of the outstanding intellectuals of his adopted country.

After winning renown in other literary fields, he produced at the age of seventy-five a highly successful drama, *La divisa punzó* (1923), based on tragic episodes of the dictatorship of Rosas, whom he pictures as the bloodthirsty tyrant of Mármol's *Amalia* written seventy years before.

Coes., *Lit. Hist.*, pp. 58–59, 105–106, 116, 146–148; Hol., pp. 491–495, 87–90

2. In Uruguay. Here the drama followed much the same course as in Argentina. There were romantic dramas concerned with the native Indians of the region, the Charrúas; plays based upon sanguinary deeds of Rosas; gaucho plays; historical dramas making patriotic appeal to the Uruguayans; and naturalistic dramas, whose best representatives were Víctor Pérez Petit and Florencio Sánchez.
   - (*a*) Víctor Pérez Petit (1871–). Poet of the *modernista* school, novelist, critic, dramatist. His influence on the social drama was marked, but many readers would prefer less emphasis upon the theme of adultery in his plays.
   - (*b*) Florencio Sánchez (1875–1910). Also identified with the Argentine theater. His dramas were presented with success in both Buenos Aires and Montevideo, usually in the same years.

Coes., *Lit. Hist.*, pp. 172, 174–176, 180–181, 192–194; Hol., pp. 489–491

3. In Chile. We have evidence of early activity in the theater in the composition and performance of the play *Hércules chileno* in Concepción in 1693. Such activity continued through the succeeding epoch — Nicolás Peña says that more than 500 plays were written in Chile up to 1912 — but we have little available information.

   Romantic Drama. After refugees from Rosas took up residence in Santiago, bringing with them the romantic movement recently introduced by Echeverría, transla-

tions of French romantic dramas were staged, notably plays of Victor Hugo and Dumas. Three Chileans were successful in original plays of this type.

(*a*) Carlos Bello (1815–1854). Oldest son of the illustrious Andrés Bello. His only play, *Los amores del poeta* (1842), was received with great enthusiasm by the public and is now considered the point of departure for the development of the modern theater in Chile, but it is a fantastic work of little merit when measured by present standards.

(*b*) Rafael Minvielle (1800–1887). Though not a native of Chile, he spent fifty years there and was identified with its literary life. His *Ernesto* (1842), staged with great acclaim a month after *Los amores del poeta*, is also significant as a foundation stone of the incipient national theater.

(*c*) Salvador Sanfuentes (1817–1860). A brilliant contemporary of Carlos Bello and a distinguished pupil of the latter's father. His poetic legends are well known, and his long drama in verse, *Juana de Nápoles* (1850), was the best of its epoch.

Historical Drama. Following closely upon the romantic plays, and with a better and more numerous representation, came the historical dramas. The following authors are outstanding.

(*a*) José Antonio Torres Arce (1828–1864). Of his four plays the most important is *La independencia de Chile*, dedicated to Salvador Sanfuentes, staged and published in 1856, and ranked as one of the best historical plays of Chile. Its popularity was heightened by the fact that the protagonist, Manuel Rodríguez, was a favorite hero of the revolution.

(*b*) Guillermo Blest Gana (1829–1904). A poet of high rank. The scene of *La conjuración de Almagro* (1858), a very successful play in verse, is Lima in 1541, and among the well-known historical characters appearing in the drama is the greatest of Peru's conquistadores, Francisco Pizarro.

(*c*) Carlos Walker Martínez (1842–1905). A highly successful and oft-repeated poetical play was his *Manuel Rodríguez* (1865), whose scene is laid in Santiago in the active revolutionary year of 1817. Its hold on the people is attested by the fact that, in addition to numerous performances, five editions of it have been published. The defects noted in its structure by critics are due chiefly to the youthfulness of the author at the time of its composition.

(*d*) Daniel Caldera (1855–1896). Considered by some critics the best dramatist of Chile. His fame rests upon *El tribunal del honor* (1877), which was so clearly based upon a real life drama in military circles that the leading characters were recognized by spectators and readers.

(*e*) Víctor Domingo Silva (1882–). Since 1908 this writer of multiple talents has produced some ten plays of varying types, social, historical, etc., among the latter *Don Alonso de Ercilla* in memory of the heroic poet-captain whose fame rests upon his American epic, *La Araucana.*

Coes., *Lit. Hist.*, pp. 199, 200, 203, 205, 212, 216–217; Hol., pp. 198–205; *Biblioteca de escritores de Chile,* vol. ix

4. In Peru. The dramatic output of this republic is in a class of its own. As love of wit and laughter has long been a characteristic of Peruvian society, the comedy has naturally been a favorite form of theatrical entertainment. No other dramatic form deserves mention.

(*a*) Felipe Pardo y Aliaga (1806–1868). Of aristocratic birth and the most prominent figure in the literary life of his day. His three comedies of national manners, marked by gay wit and subtle irony, won great favor among his contemporaries. The first one, *Los frutos de la educación* (1829), ridicules in a delightful manner the age-old custom of parents' choosing husbands for their daughters.

(*b*) Manuel Ascencio Segura (1805–1871). His twelve comedies, though appearing more than ten years after Pardo's first success, reveal and play to the same fun-loving Peruvian society. He was a closer observer as well as a better craftsman than Pardo.

Coes., *Lit. Hist.*, pp. 246, 247; Hol., pp. 440–445

5. In Mexico. Many authors have tried their hand at play writing in all epochs, but not many have won enduring fame. Manuel Acuña, for instance, wrote one play which was successful on the stage for some time, *El pasado*, on the theme of the social rehabilitation of fallen women. At various times there has been a dramatic revival, the latest being since 1920, in which the younger men have been active. Among the latter are Francisco Monterde G. I. with *La que volvió a la vida* and several other plays, Jiménez Rueda with *Como en la vida*, etc., and other less well-known writers of the day.

(*a*) Manuel Eduardo de Gorostiza (1789–1851). He is often credited with having introduced the modern drama into his native country, but his comedies are usually identified with Spanish literature because of his long residence in Spain, where his plays were written and staged from 1818 to 1833. *Indulgencia para todos* (1818) is the best of his production, but *Contigo pan y cebolla* (1833), inciting laughter at the expense of silly, romantic girls, has always been the most popular.

(*b*) Ignacio Rodríguez Galván (1816–1842). See 8*a*, p. 32. Also of colonial inspiration is *El privado del virrey*, enacted not long after the *Muñoz*.

(*c*) Fernando Calderón y Beltrán (1809–1845). See 8*b*, p. 34. His best drama, the historical tragedy *Ana Bolena*, shows fine character drawing. Many critics have praised *A ninguna de las tres* for its excellent comic characters and good dialogue.

(*d*) José Peón y Contreras (1843–1909). The most successful and popular of the dramatists who brought

about a revival of the theater after Porfirio Díaz became president. Had he written less rapidly and with more care his place in dramatic literature would be higher than it is. His numerous plays belong to the romantic school, Zorrilla and Echegaray being his models.

(*e*) Rafael Delgado (1853–1914). Author of two plays prominent in the dramatic revival, being rewarded for one of them with a silver crown. His literary fame, however, rests more securely upon his novels. See p. 94, 9*a*.

(*f*) Marcelino Dávalos (?–). His nine plays, based on national life, have appeared since 1900. He is one of the dramatists who have aroused renewed interest in the theater in the last fifteen years.

(*g*) Julio Jiménez Rueda (1896–). One of Mexico's widely known living writers. Possessing considerable talent and culture, as well as a prolific pen, he has won recognition in several fields. His half dozen plays to date hold an important place in the contemporary dramatic revival.

Coes., *Lit. Hist.*, pp. 350, 335–338, 357–360, 367–369; Hol., pp. 399–404; Jim. R., pp. 193, 126–129, 148–151, 197, 230–232

THE NOVEL

During the colonial epoch the Laws of the Indies forbade the importation into America of "historias fingidas," particularly of the novels of chivalry that were popular in Spain at the beginning of the conquest of the New World. Not before the 19th century, apparently, was any serious attempt made to produce fiction. The picaresque novel of José Joaquín Fernández de Lizardi, *El Periquillo Sarniento* (1816), important for its place in the revolutionary period (page 14), may be taken as the pioneer novel of Spanish America.

A. Nineteenth Century Novelists

1. In Argentina. During the tyranny of Rosas the importation of foreign novels began, but before the battle

of Caseros none was printed in this country. After the organization of the republic under Mitre and Sarmiento foreign novels, like those of Balzac, Zola, Daudet, and others, were imported in greater numbers, and the genre gradually developed among Argentinian writers. By 1880, a reading public with a taste for novels being definitely established, fiction began to flourish.

(*a*) José Mármol (1817–1871). See p. 18. As Mármol was in exile in Montevideo, his *Amalia* was published there in 1852. While not a work of great literary merit, it is still widely read for its intense narrative interest.

(*b*) Eduardo Gutiérrez (1853–1890). See 10, p. 22.

(*c*) Eugenio Cambaceres (1843–1888). A disciple of Zola. Because of his clear-cut pictures of life in the capital and on the Pampa some critics have called him the founder of the national novel. His four novels, produced between 1880 and 1887, were *Silbidos de un vago*, *Sin rumbo*, *Música sentimental*, and *En la sangre*.

(*d*) Pablo Groussac (1848–1929). See 1*f*, p. 58. To his realistic novel, *Fruto vedado* (1884), a study of political and social life in Buenos Aires, he owes his fame as a novelist.

(*e*) Carlos María Ocantos (1860– ?). The initiator of the South American realistic school of novelists and often called the Argentine Balzac. In his considerable production are found, from 1888 to 1929, twenty Argentine novels, six Spanish, and six Danish. With his multiple talents he played the rôle of close observer, critic, delicate satirist, psychologist, philologist, and educator. He is at his best in the novel of character. As his later years were spent in Madrid he was not closely identified with the contemporary literary world of Argentina. *León Zaldívar*, *Promisión*, *La Ginesa*, *Don Perfecto*, and *El peligro* are among the best known of his novels.

Coes., *Lit. Hist.*, pp. 114, 162–166; Hol., pp. 16–18, 58–60;

87, 62–63; Tor., *Ant.*,.3–8, *La nov.*, pp. 190–192, 205, 218, 202

2. In Uruguay. As in other literary forms, the novel of Uruguay is closely related in type and theme to that of her sister republic.

   (*a*) Alejandro Magariños Cervantes (1825–1893). See 1*a*, p. 24. A disciple of Echeverría and the first of his country to make his production genuinely South American. His first novel was *La estrella del sur*. His poetic *Celiar* is really a gaucho novel.

   (*b*) Eduardo Acevedo Díaz (1851–1921). The greatest Uruguayan novelist. His first novel was *Brenda* (1884), romantic with realistic episodes. It was followed by a historical trilogy depicting gaucho life: *Ismael* (1888), *Nativa*, and *El grito de gloria*, all three being naturalistic. *Soledad*, thoroughly naturalistic, is also concerned with gaucho life. The last novels of Acevedo Díaz were *Minés* and *Lanza y sable*.

   (*c*) Carlos Reyles (1868–1938). The master of Uruguayan naturalists. *Por la vida* (1888) was unimportant. But *Beba* (1894) is a strong national novel which presents a study of life on a large cattle ranch. *La raza de Caín* (1900) contains repulsive details concerning mental and moral degenerates. The later novels of Reyles belong to another type and generation.

   (*d*) Javier de Viana (1872–1926). His novels, *Campo* (1896), *Gaucha* (1899), and others, belong to the realism of the 19th century. They picture the gaucho as a degenerate and weakling who is being submerged in national life. In his later production Viana was an unequaled storyteller belonging to another generation.

Coes., *Lit. Hist.*, pp. 176–179, 187–192; Hol., pp. 472–480; Tor., *Ant.*, pp. 21–30, *La nov.*, pp. 193, 206, 213–215

3. In Chile. Since the middle of the 19th century novelists have been active in Chile. Of the many whose works

still endure the following are most worthy of mention. As the first novel written by a Chilean was published in Lima (*El Inquisidor Mayor o Historia de unos amores*, 1852) and depicts the society of that city, it really belongs to the literary production of Peru. Manuel Bilbao was its author.

(*a*) Alberto Blest Gana (1831–1922). The greatest of the Chilean novelists, called the American Balzac. His sixteen social and historical novels, twelve of them published from 1858 to 1864, were an important contribution to Chilean literature. In his masterpiece, *Martín Rivas* (1862), Blest Gana is seen at his best as a teacher of morals and a critic of contemporary society. After a gap of thirty years in his literary activity he returned to novel writing with the same powers of keen observation and vigorous delineation of character. As he never forsook his first manner his entire production belongs in spirit to the 19th century.

(*b*) Daniel Barros Grez (1839–1904). Author of Chile's greatest historical novel, *Pipiolos y Pelucones* (1876). Modeled after Walter Scott, it gives a vivid and detailed account of the struggle between Chile's rival political parties during the thirties. Another long novel, *El Huérfano* (1881), in the picaresque manner, portrays the life of all classes of Chilean society. A novel of political customs, *La Academia político-literaria* (1890), and a long but very popular series of adventures of his dog entitled *Primeras aventuras del perro Cuatro Remos en Santiago* (1898), complete his list of fiction.

(*c*) Vicente Grez (1843–1909). A disciple of Zola, he published in quick succession four novels upon which his modest fame rests: *Emilia Reynals* (1883), *La dote de una joven* (1884), *Marianita* (1885), and *El ideal de una esposa* (1887).

Coes., *Lit. Hist.*, pp. 224–228, 231–233; Hol., pp. 165–169; Tor., *Ant.*, pp. 9–14, *La nov.*, pp. 197, 221

4. In Peru. The most important early novelists in Peru were women, of whom two are outstanding.

   (a) Clorinda Matto de Turner (1854–1909). Widely known for her famous *Aves sin nido* (1889), a powerful social novel depicting the deplorable state of the Indian economically, socially, and otherwise. The book is a stinging indictment of both church and state for their shameless exploitation of the indigenous population. Among the other novels of Señora Turner, not well known, are *Índole* (1891) and *Herencia.*

   (b) Mercedes Cabello de Carbonera (?). Her novels, which give varied realistic pictures of Peruvian society and deal with problems of the day, are *Las consecuencias* (1889), *El conspirador* (1892), and *Blanca Sol* (1889). The latter, a study of woman in high social circles in Lima, was long popular.

Coes., *Lit. Hist.*, pp. 258–260; Tor., *La nov.*, pp. 194, 225, 207

5. In Ecuador. The outstanding romantic poet of Ecuador, Juan León Mera (1832–1899), produced the country's best novel of the 19th century and probably the best of all Spanish American novels with an Indian heroine, *Cumandá* (1879). With this vigorous, tragic work Mera sustained his reputation of " poeta indiano " that he won with his poetic legend, *La virgen del sol* (1861), and also received high praise from several foreign critics.

Coes., *Lit. Hist.*, pp. 270–271; Hol., pp. 334–336; Tor., *La nov.*, pp. 193, 229

6. In Colombia. Here both romanticism and realism found expression in the novel.

   (a) Jorge Isaacs (1837–1895). The natural beauties of Colombian landscape which have inspired numerous poets are pictured in the most widely read work of fiction written in Spanish America in the 19th century, *María* (1867). See 6*e*, p. 30.

(*b*) Lorenzo Marroquín (1856–1918). Of wholly different type from the romantic *María* is his realistic *Pax* (1907), a vibrant study of the political and social conditions of his day which aroused indignation at home and established his fame abroad.

Coes., *Lit. Hist.*, pp. 300–302; Hol., pp. 242–244; Tor., *Ant.*, pp. 15–20, *La nov.*, pp. 194–196, 203

7. In Venezuela. The followers of Zola left no imperishable novel to Venezuelan literature, but out of the naturalistic school developed the nationalistic or *criollo* movement which produced better fiction.
   (*a*) Manuel Romero García (1865–). His *Peonía* (1890) launched the new movement with a vivid picture of abuses in the existing social order. *Marcelo* and *Acuarela* are other novels of the same type.
   (*b*) Gonzalo Picón Febres (1860–1918). *El sargento Felipe* (1899) is unsurpassed among the *criollo* novels, full of unforgettable details of Venezuelan life and glimpses into the soul of the creole.
   (*c*) Miguel Eduardo Pardo (1868–1905). His satirical novel *Todo un pueblo* met great success. It breathes hatred and scorn for customs and ideas of which he felt himself a victim.

Coes., *Lit. Hist.*, pp. 326, 329–332; Hol., 519–523, 525-527; Tor., *Ant.*, pp. 240, 207

8. In Mexico. Mexican romantic fiction, abundant and usually in imitation of the French, is of little distinction. Later schools, however, had a strong representation in the republic and left more lasting productions.
   (*a*) Justo Sierra (1814–1861). In 1841 he published *Un año en el hospital de San Lázaro*, a novel in the form of letters. Of more merit is *La hija del Judío*, based on historical incidents in Yucatán.
   (*b*) Manuel Payno (1810–1894). *El fistol del diablo* (1845), the first novel published by a follower of Fernández de Lizardi, and like the *Periquillo* a study of Mexican social classes, was received by the

reading public with almost as much acclaim as its model. *Los bandidos de Río Frío* (1888) is much superior in literary quality to *El fistol*, but has been less popular.

(*c*) Juan Díaz Covarrubias (1837–1859). In his brief, tragic life he wrote a historical novel which gives him a definite place in Mexican letters: *Gil Gómez el Insurgente*, a story of Hidalgo's first activities in the war for independence.

(*d*) Ignacio Manuel Altamirano (1834–1893). *Clemencia*, a semi-historical novel, was popular in its time and is still read frequently; *El Zarco* has met less favor; while *La Navidad en las montañas*, a charming poetic tale picturing an episode of rural life in the mountains, is widely used in schools, especially in the United States.

(*e*) Juan Antonio Mateos (?). Widely read but of inferior quality are his realistic novels, the best of which is *Cerro de las Campanas*, a historical novel narrating sympathetically the tragic end of ill-fated Maximilian.

(*f*) Vicente Riva Palacio (1832–1896). As he was a ranking literary figure and the Mexican general to whom Maximilian surrendered, Riva Palacio's story of the fallen Emperor in *Calvario y Tabor* received great popular favor, though critics assert that the novelist did not use his materials to the best advantage. Other novels which came from his pen aroused less interest.

Coes., *Lit. Hist.*, pp. 343, 345–348, 352, 354–355; Hol., p. 355; Tor., *La nov.*, p. 200; Ros.-Tem., *Prose*, pp. 29–34

9. In Santo Domingo. The long cultural tradition of the Dominican Republic has not received adequate recognition among students of New World literature. With a university founded in 1558, a high degree of culture existed in the island from colonial times and its influence has been widespread. The novel, as well as other literary forms, has had worthy representatives here.

Manuel de Jesús Galván (1834–1911). Author of one of the best historical novels written in Spanish America, *Enriquillo* (1882). Diego Colón, a son of Columbus, and the illustrious Fray Bartolomé de las Casas are among the characters in the novel, which ranks high among the " novelas indianistas."

Coes., *Lit. Hist.*, p. 435; Tor., *La nov.*, p. 193 (For an excellent treatment of this novel see *La novela indianista* of Concha Meléndez.)

B. The Contemporary Novel (1900–1930). Since 1900 there has been a steady growth of interest in and production of novels in all parts of Spanish America. No literary form is more widely cultivated at present. The most original and most truly American novels are those which present studies of rural life, the predominating type being the regional novel. And the most highly esteemed are those, not too localized, which can be read in any country without losing anything of their plot or action.

1. In Argentina. The artistic novel with national setting and atmosphere appeared with the generation of the review *Ideas* in 1900. Up to 1920 Argentine literature continued to be strongly influenced by French models and ideas, but since that year the nationalization of the novel has been marked. National problems and ideals, native landscapes, and American atmosphere and culture have become dominant, fulfilling the early dream of Echeverría for the Americanization of Argentine literature.

(*a*) César Duayen (?). Her only novel, *Stella* (1905), ranks high as a picture of the social customs of the wealthy class of Buenos Aires. Permeated by the pathos of the brief life of an angelic crippled child, the novel holds before the capital's high society a mirror in which are revealed the moral and educational shortcomings of both old and young. In spite of its length and multiplicity of details, *Stella* holds the reader's interest at high pitch to the end.

(*b*) Roberto J. Payró (1867–1928). One of the first to turn from French influence and nationalize the novel. His masterpiece, a picaresque novel of rural life, *El casamiento de Laucha* (1906), ranks among the best novels of his country. He is also a realist in *Pago chico* (1908) and *Las divertidas aventuras del nieto de Juan Moreira* (1910). He wrote four problem plays, in which he did not reach the height attained in his novels.

(*c*) Enrique Rodríguez Larreta (1875–). His masterpiece, *La gloria de don Ramiro* (1911), is unfortunately not American, but an artistic, masterly picture of Toledo in the time of Philip II. Fifteen years later appeared *Zogoibi*, a tale of gaucho life on an *estancia* in Argentina which lacks the artistic merits of its predecessor as well as feeling for the spiritual values of the Pampa.

(*d*) Manuel Gálvez (1882–). One of the editors of *Ideas* and an educator who left a deep impression on Argentina's educational system. Two of his novels, *La maestra normal* (1914) and *La sombra del convento* (1917), are among the most artistic that Argentina has produced. The sincerity of Gálvez' feeling for native landscape and the vigorous, sentimental touch with which he depicts the manners and customs of the provinces of the republic are among his outstanding virtues as a novelist. His three novels based on the war of Paraguay, *Los caminos de la muerte* (1928), *Humaitá* (1929), and *Jornadas de agonía*, are unexcelled in America for their dramatic force and their penetrating psychology. Of his *Nacha Regules* (1919), a story of the redemption of a woman of the streets, he published also a dramatized version. Several other realistic novels complete his work in fiction and established his place in Spanish American letters.

(*e*) Benito Lynch (1885–). A novelist of rural life who understands and sympathizes with the humble people of the Pampa. *Los caranchos de la Florida*

is a powerful picture of the sufferings of the dependents on the Florida *estancia* at the hands of its cruel, devouring owners, "the vultures," whose heartless deeds of violence cost them their lives through murder. *El inglés de los güesos* paints the reaction of the natives to a foreign student of fossils whose occupation is beyond their comprehension. Three other less vigorous novels complete Lynch's output.

(*f*) Ricardo Güiraldes (1886–1927). For many critics his *Don Segundo Sombra* (1927) is a belated masterpiece of the gaucho school that holds high rank among Spanish American novels. But it must be granted that in point of artistic merit and through lack of any spiritual conception of the landscape this novel is inferior to *Xamaica* (1923), which is in fact the author's best production, though less widely accepted and applauded. The distinctive merit of *Don Segundo Sombra* is the vividness of the central figure, a son of the Pampa, around whom the episodes of the novel revolve. *Raucho* (1917) and *Rosaura* (1923) add little to the novelist's fame.

(*g*) "Hugo Wast" — Gustavo Martínez Zuviría (1883–). Most prolific of Argentine novelists. With a series of twenty novels published from 1902 to 1929, some of them with phenomenal sales at home and abroad, no Spanish American writer has met greater financial success. Despite the defects of style and composition to which critics point an accusing finger, Wast's novels have continued to arouse the interest of the public and to be best sellers. Ranking highest for their artistic values, psychological analysis, and excellent description are *Fuente sellada* (1914), *Valle negro* (1916), and *Desierto de piedra* (1925). *Flor de durazno* (1911) has sold more than a hundred thousand copies, though it is not one of Wast's best productions.

Coes., *Lit. Hist.*, pp. 167, 168, 493, 494, 497–500; Hol., pp. 64, 67–78; Tor., *Ant.*, pp. 34–38, 43–49, 58–66, 73–78, *La nov.*, pp. 206, 218–221

2. In Uruguay. Following the manner of Acevedo Díaz and Javier de Viana at the close of the 19th century there is another important novelist inspired by gaucho themes and also minor novelists who have produced a half dozen readable works of the same type since 1920.

   (*a*) Justino Zavala Muniz (1897–). His thoroughly realistic work dealing with the gaucho life of the past is found in his three *crónicas: Crónica de Muniz* (1921), the biography of his grandfather, a celebrated *caudillo* of earlier days; *Crónica de un crimen* (1926), a study of rural Uruguay in the period following the disappearance of the great *caudillos*, when the gaucho degenerated into a criminal; *Crónica de la reja* (1930), more truly a novel, an artistic novel which glorifies the peaceful life and honest work of the simple laborer who is the present descendent of the nobler gaucho of the first period.

   (*b*) Horacio Quiroga (1878–1937). A native of Uruguay, he spent most of his life in Argentina and is identified with its literature. In his fiction, which takes the form of tales rather than novels, nature is frequently the dominant character, now as a hostile animal, again as a devastating flood. Poe's influence in his stories is marked. *Anaconda* (1921) is representative of his best symbolical and philosophical work.

Coes., *Lit. Hist.*, p. 496; Hol., p. 480; Tor., *Ant.*, p. 94, *La nov.*, pp. 215–217, 220

3. In Chile. Among the literary men of recent years in Chile good story writers have been numerous and prominent, for example, Mariano Latorre with his regional types. (See Tor., *La nov.*, pp. 222–224.) A few authors may be classed more definitely as novelists.

   (*a*) Eduardo Barrios (1884–). An outstanding figure in novel and drama, preferring psychological themes and treatment. Well known for his *El*

hermano asno (1926), a humorous narrative of the life of the protagonist in a monastery, and *Un perdido* (1917), a character study of a young man in army life. The latter has been called the best psychological novel produced in Chile.

(*b*) "F. Santiván"—Fernando Santibáñez (1886–). Author of tales and novels of rural life. Delineation of character is a strong feature of his work, especially in *La hechizada* (1916), in which he lays bare the soul of a country-bred girl.

(*c*) Pedro Prado (1886–). His best novel is *Alsino* (1920), a symbolical and fantastic story in which a boy learns to fly. His place is secure among the writers who have made studies of Chilean life. Besides three novels he has published several collections of verse and of "prose poems."

Coes., *Lit. Hist.*, pp. 477, 490–492; Hol., p. 171; Tor., *Ant.*, pp. 53, 67, *La nov.*, pp. 222–224, *G. N. de A.*

4. In Bolivia. During the last twenty years interest in the indigenous population of Bolivia has become prominent in fiction. The principal novelist is Alcides Arguedas (1879–), whose most significant work is *Raza de bronce* (1919), dealing with moral and ethnical problems concerning the Bolivian Indian, who is portrayed against the native landscape. In an earlier novel, *Wuata Wuara* (1904), Arguedas had forcefully presented the tragedies connected with the life of a mistreated Indian girl who was the "flor de su raza y de su tierra." *Vida criolla* (1912) describes life in La Paz.

Hol., p. 109; Tor., *Ant.*, p. 39, *La nov.*, pp. 225–227

5. In Peru. Following a path indicated by Abraham Valdelomar (1888–1919) before his untimely death, numerous novelists have been inspired by the rich Incan traditions and the life of the natives of the Andean region. The definitive novel of this type is yet to be written. Of considerable merit is *La serpiente de*

oro (1935), a prize-winning novel published in Santiago by Ciro Alegría. In this novel, which deals with the Peruvian *cholos*, the Marañón river is the all but human protagonist, absolutely dominating the existence upon its banks: "We *cholos* of the Marañón listen to its voice with attentive ear. We do not know the source or the end of this river which would destroy us if we tried to gauge it in our reed boats, but its voice speaks to us clearly from its immensity."

Hol., p. 426; Tor., *La nov.*, pp. 227–229

6. In Ecuador. In the last dozen years the novel concerned with the exploitation of the Indians has become popular also in Ecuador. Several of the younger writers, born in this century, — Fernando Chaves, Demetrio Aguilera Malta, José de la Cuadra, and others — are busy in this field. The novelist who is protesting most earnestly with his pen is Jorge Icaza. His *Huasipungo* (1934) pictures the brutal injustice shown the Indian in the rural areas, while *En las calles*, a prize winner of 1935, does the same service for the wretched natives exploited in factories.

Tor., *La nov.*, pp. 229–236

7. In Colombia. The Colombian novelist most widely acclaimed in this century is José Eustacio Rivera (1889–1928), author of *La vorágine* (1924), a regional novel which gives a powerful description of the tragic lives of the rubber gatherers of the selvas.

Tor., *Ant.*, p. 79

8. In Venezuela. Three Venezuelan novelists of wholly different genius and inspiration rank high among Spanish America's men of letters.

   (*a*) Rufino Blanco Fombona (1874–). His satire on politicians in 1916, *El hombre de oro*, which was preceded in 1905 by a picture of the anarchic conditions in Venezuela, *El hombre de hierro*, marked him as a master of satirical protest against a regime which he

opposed at the risk of his life. His caustic criticism fell freely on the clergy in *La mitra en la mano* (1927). Possessing many talents and a prolific pen, Blanco Fombona has made vital contributions to other fields besides the novel.

(*b*) Rómulo Gallegos (1884–). Praised for the perfection of his technique and ranked among the three greatest American novelists, he owes much of his fame to *Doña Bárbara* (1929), which is considered by some critics the best novel written in Latin America. It describes life in a southwestern plain of Venezuela where the landscape exerts a malignant influence upon man and the climate makes him a brute and a criminal: " La llanura es la devoradora de hombres."

(*c*) Teresa de la Parra (1895–1936). Fame came to her with her first novel, *Ifigenia* (1924), a prize winner. She is better known in the United States for *Las memorias de Mamá Blanca*, pleasing sketches of country life in Venezuela.

Coes., *Lit. Hist.*, pp. 327–329, 487; Hol., pp. 529, 537; Tor., *Ant.*, p. 50, *G. N. de A.*

9. In Mexico. Mariano Azuela's *Los de abajo* (1916), translated into English with the title *The under dogs*, initiated a type of novel which has been widely cultivated in recent years. But no other writer has equaled the master, and few works of the group will live except possibly as books giving data on the era in Mexico called " La revolución." Azuela (1873–) has published ten books and continues active, but *Los de abajo* is to date his most important production. The novelists of this group are continuing the tradition established by the following realists and naturalists who preceded them, and who may rightly be called the precursors of the " novela de revolución."

(*a*) Rafael Delgado (1853–1914). Sometimes called the Mexican Pereda. One of the best Mexican

realists, though *Angelina* (1895) is a definitely romantic novel showing the influence of Isaacs' *María*. *La Calandria* (1891), his masterpiece, is a psychological study of lower class morals and manners which is full of tragic pathos. The satirical *Los parientes ricos* (1903) pictures the middle class. See 5e, p. 68.

(*b*) José López Portillo y Rojas (1850–1923). His best novel, *La parcela* (1898), describes the struggle of two wealthy landowners for the possession of a plot of ground. Much of the value of the novel lies in its pictures of rural life in Jalisco. Also a portrayal of ranch life is *Fuertes y débiles* (1919), revealing deep-lying causes of revolution in Mexico. *Los precursores* (1909) likewise deals with national life.

(*c*) Federico Gamboa (1864–1939). A naturalist after the manner of Zola. The bulk of his work belongs to the 19th century, but *Santa* (1903), most widely known of his novels, and *La llaga* (1910) place him among the contemporaries. His four dramas, though favorably received, have brought him less fame than his fiction.

Coes., *Lit. Hist.*, pp. 366–372; Hol., pp. 382–387; Tor., *Ant.*, p. 31, *La nov.*, pp. 200, 201, 207, *G. N. de A.;* Ros.-Tem., *Prose*, pp. 44–54

10. In Guatemala. This small republic, which has had poets of merit from colonial days to the present, has today a distinguished writer who is both poet and novelist, Rafael Arévalo Martínez (1884–). His *El hombre que parecía un caballo* (1915) is probably the best known of his several fascinating tales in which he depicts the animal aspect in human beings.

Hol., p. 131; Tor., *Ant.*, p. 107

11. In Cuba. This century finds the novel widely cultivated in Cuba by a group of minor writers using native themes. The Spanish American novelist who had most of the spirit of Zola was born in the lower classes, Carlos

Loveira (1882–1929). His work, at least partly biographical, reflects the vulgar mind and manners of the class to which the author belonged. His best novel, *Juan Criollo* (1927), depicts vividly the social and political corruption rife in Cuba at the close of the last century. *Los ciegos* (1922) is socialistic, as is much of his other work, and all but violently anticlerical. *Generales y doctores* (1920) is an attack upon the political degradation immediately preceding the Spanish American war. All the novels of Loveira contain details for the study of social and political conditions in Cuba.

Coes., *Lit. Hist.*, pp. 487–489; Hol., p. 293; Tor., *La nov.*, pp. 207–209, 240–242

12. In Santo Domingo. Tulio M. Cestero (1877–). In his early writings an extravagant modernist but more restrained in his later and better works. His vigorous novel *La sangre* (1913) deals with the bloody dictatorship of a tyrant president, Ulises Heureaux.

Coes., *Lit. Hist.*, p. 437; Hol., p. 318; Tor., *La nov.*, pp. 164, 243

OTHER DISTINGUISHED PROSE WRITERS

Coming under no category thus far given in this outline survey are numerous excellent prose writers of continental renown who represent the best in their respective fields, of whom at least the following should be noted.

1. Juan Montalvo (1833–1889) of Ecuador. An implacable critic of political tyrants and a caustic enemy of the clergy. In literature his flawless Castilian and unique style are seen at their best in *Siete tratados* and *Capítulos que se le olvidaron a Cervantes*, the former a series of brilliant essays on nobility, beauty, genius, and other topics, and the latter a notable imitation of the style and spirit of Cervantes in *Don Quijote*.
2. Benjamín Vicuña Mackenna (1831–1886) of Chile. The

most notable historian and most prolific writer of America, author of one hundred and sixty volumes. Active in political and diplomatic life, he felt a personal interest in every epoch of Chilean history.

3. Eugenio María de Hostos (1839–1903). A Puerto Rican of continental caliber who spent much of his life in exile. His influence was especially great in Santo Domingo, where he did important work in organizing the school system, and in Chile, where he was professor of international law in the national university. Of his varied writings on pedagogy, sociology, ethics, law, and other subjects, the highest place belongs to his *Lecciones de derecho constitucional.* A definitive biography of this great man of 19th-century Spanish America will probably result from the offer of two $1000 prizes for such a work made by the De Hostos Centenary Commission of Puerto Rico in 1939.

   Coes., *Lit. Hist.*, p. 442; Hol., p. 314

4. Rufino José Cuervo (1844–1911) of Colombia. An eminent philologist whose grammatical studies in Spanish and in Latin brought him international renown. Best known in the United States for his authoritative *Notas a la gramática castellana de D. Andrés Bello*, of which there have been seventeen editions. Cuervo was also a poet of much talent.
5. Ricardo Palma (1833–1919) of Peru. The inimitable *tradicionista* who left an imperishable impression upon Spanish American letters. As the self-appointed chronicler of Peruvian life from colonial days to the War of the Pacific, he wrote his nine series of richly humorous *Tradiciones peruanas* from 1872 to 1906, and won the rank of the greatest figure in Peruvian literature.
6. José Toribio Medina (1852–1930) of Chile. Pre-eminent critic and historian, author of a very long list of notable and authoritative works ranging from the history of printing in all the Spanish American colonies to the *Historia de la literatura colonial de Chile* and a critical edition of Pedro de Oña's *Arauco domado.*
7. Ricardo Rojas (1882–) of Argentina. Former rector of the National University of Buenos Aires, he has written

copiously, — at least five volumes of poetry besides a drama and double this number in various types of prose. His four-volume *La literatura argentina* (1917–1922) contains a wealth of details gathered in his years of research.

Coes., *Lit. Hist.*, pp. 266–268, 240, 303, 254–257, 242, 491; Hol., pp. 337, 186, 253, 423, 190, 46; Weis., pp. 129–154; Tor., *Ant.*, pp. 87, 125, *La nov.*, pp. 229, 198

POETS OF THE "NEW GENERATION" (1910–)

The close of the first decade of the twentieth century found poetry shifting from "Art for Art's sake" and artificiality to a more serious attitude toward the realities of life. Verse became more simple and direct. Emotional appeal replaced rhetorical adornment. The poet looked for the inner meaning of things, the hidden truth which he might interpret. Many of the new poets discarded rhyme and employed assonance or free verse. Later a few of the more erratic resorted to a fantastic arrangement of lines on the page, and others of the radicals wished to abolish syntax and signs of punctuation. Several *isms* found their way into the nomenclature of the various vanguard groups, like futurism, ultraism, cubism, dadaism, and creationism.

1. Gabriela Mistral (1889–). Native of Chile who has won continental fame by her verse rather than by her numerous educational and diplomatic activities. *Desolación* (1922) contains her best production. Sympathy for the poor, in particular for underprivileged women and children, is one of her strong characteristics. Much of her verse is very simple, tender, and sad, and there is often a marked religious mysticism present.
2. Pedro Prado (1886–). Also a Chilean. One of the best contemporary lyric poets. Fond of free verse and assonance. One of his best-known poems is *Lázaro*, an expression of the poet's materialistic ideas. See 3c, p. 90.
3. Enrique Banchs (1888–). Argentine poet of classic tendencies, free from rhetorical adornment. His verse is marked by sincerity and naturalness. His five volumes of poetry have been published in Buenos Aires since 1907.

4. Alfonsina Storni (1892–1938). A gifted Argentine teacher in whose verse the theme of earthly love is predominant. She voices her disappointment with the world and with life in genuine, American poetry.
5. Vicente Huidobro (1893–). Chilean. A creationist and representative of the more advanced ideas and practices of the "new generation," perhaps because of his associations in his long residence in Paris. To the average reader some of his verse is senseless. He is one of those who wish to discard punctuation along with everything else conventional in writing.
6. Juana de Ibarbourou (1895–). Uruguay's leading woman poet, who has been called the greatest of the women writing in Spanish today. Love of life and country are strong in her verse. Extraordinarily sensitive to the appeal of nature, she expresses herself in lyrics full of sincerity and originality. Seven editions of her poems have been published, the first in 1918.
7. Jorge Luis Borges (1900–). By his own confession a standard bearer of ultraism. Claiming absolute freedom for the poet, he uses as he pleases rhyme or free verse, traditional forms or those of his own invention. In all cases emotion must dominate rhythm and metrics. Yet he presents life sympathetically and is a good representative of Americanism.

Coes., *Lit. Hist.*, pp. 482–486; Hol., pp. 155–162, 50, 53–55, 462; Tor., *Ant.*, pp. 204, 196, 207; Craig, pp. 194–205, 320, 154–167, 313, 174–181, 317, 236–247, 334–338; Solar, pp. 229–244

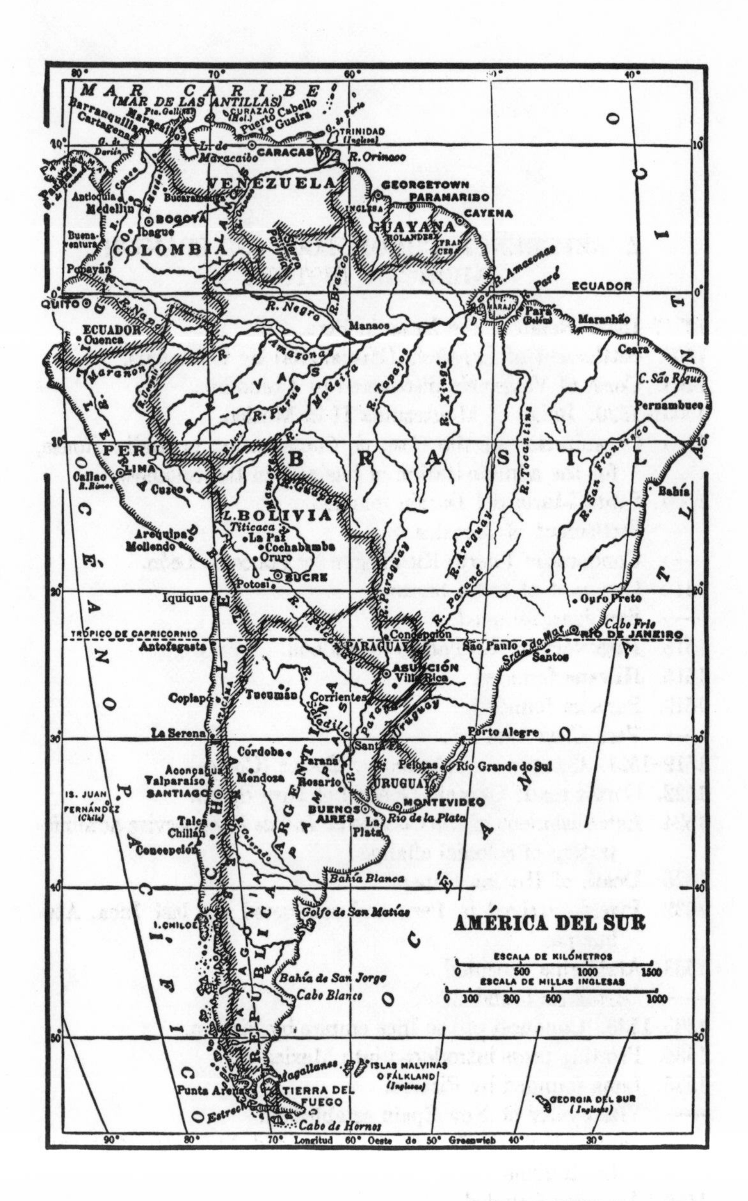

MAR CARIBE
(MAR DE LAS ANTILLAS)
Barranquilla
Cartagena
Maracaibo
Pta. Gallinas
CURAZAO (Hol.)
Puerto Cabello
La Guaira
G. de Paria
TRINIDAD (Inglesa)
G. de Darién
L. de Maracaibo
CARACAS
R. Orinoco
VENEZUELA
GEORGETOWN
PARAMARIBO
CAYENA
Antioquia
Medellín
Bucaramanga
BOGOTÁ
Ibague
GUAYANA
INGLESA
HOLANDESA
FRANCESA
Buenaventura
COLOMBIA
Popayán
R. Amazonas
Pará
ECUADOR
QUITO
R. Napo
ECUADOR
Cuenca
R. Negro
Manaos
R. Branco
Pará (Belém)
Maranhão
Ceará
C. São Roque
Pernambuco
R. Marañon
R. Purus
R. Madeira
R. Tapajos
R. Xingú
R. Tocantins
BRASIL
PERÚ
LIMA
Callao
R. Rímac
Cuzco
R. Guaporé
R. San Francisco
Bahía
L. Titicaca
BOLIVIA
La Paz
Cochabamba
Oruro
Arequipa
Mollendo
Potosí
SUCRE
R. Araguay
R. Paraná
R. Paraguay
Iquique
Ouro Preto
Cabo Frío
TRÓPICO DE CAPRICORNIO
Antofagasta
Concepción
PARAGUAY
São Paulo
RÍO DE JANEIRO
Santos
ASUNCIÓN
Villa Rica
Copiapó
Tucumán
Corrientes
R. Uruguay
La Serena
Porto Alegre
Santa Fe
Córdoba
Paraná
Pelotas
Río Grande do Sul
Aconcagua
Valparaíso
SANTIAGO
Mendoza
Rosario
URUGUAY
MONTEVIDEO
IS. JUAN FERNÁNDEZ (Chile)
BUENOS AIRES
La Plata
Río de la Plata
Talca
Chillán
Concepción
R. Colorado
Bahía Blanca
Golfo de San Matías
I. CHILOÉ
AMÉRICA DEL SUR
ESCALA DE KILÓMETROS
0 500 1000 1500
ESCALA DE MILLAS INGLESAS
0 100 300 500 1000
Bahía de San Jorge
Cabo Blanco
ISLAS MALVINAS O FÁLKLAND (Inglesas)
Magallanes
Punta Arenas
TIERRA DEL FUEGO
Estrecho
Cabo de Hornos
GEORGIA DEL SUR (Inglesas)
OCÉANO PACÍFICO
OCÉANO ATLÁNTICO
REPÚBLICA ARGENTINA
PATAGONIA
PAMPAS
90° 80° 70° Longitud 60° Oeste de 50° Greenwich 40° 30°

A REFERENCE CHRONOLOGY OF SPANISH AMERICAN HISTORY

1021?–1532. Reign of the Incas in Peru.
1493. Settlement of Española (Hispaniola) by Columbus.
1498. Coast of Venezuela discovered by Columbus.
1503?–1520. Reign of Montezuma II in Mexico.
1503. Organization of the *Casa de Contratación*, or India House, for the administration of business in the colonies.
1509. Santa María del Darién founded.
—— Settlement of Jamaica.
—— Conquest of Puerto Rico begun by Ponce de León.
1511. Conquest of Cuba began.
—— San Juan founded.
1513. Discovery of the Pacific by Balboa.
1515. Havana founded.
1519. Panama founded.
—— Vera Cruz founded.
1519–1521. Conquest of Mexico by Cortez (Cortés).
1522. Cortez made Captain-General of New Spain.
1524. Establishment of the *Consejo de Indias* to supervise administration of colonial affairs.
1525. Death of Huaina Capac.
1532. Pizarro arrived in Peru and conquered the last Inca, Atahualpa.
1533. Atahualpa executed.
—— Cartagena founded.
1533–1535. Conquest of the Inca empire by Pizarro.
1534. Printing press introduced into Mexico.
1535. Lima founded by Pizarro.
—— Viceroyalty of New Spain established.
—— Santa María de Buenos Aires founded, but later destroyed by Indians.
1536. Asunción founded.

1538. University of Santo Tomás de Aquino founded in Santo Domingo (Española).
—— Santa Fe de Bogotá founded.
1541. Santiago founded in Chile.
—— Pizarro assassinated in Lima.
1544. Viceroyalty established in Peru.
1545. Potosí established.
1547. Cortez died in Spain.
1548. La Paz founded.
1551. Universities of Mexico and San Marcos in Lima established.
1557. García Hurtado de Mendoza made Captain-General of Chile.
1567. Santiago de León de Caracas founded.
1579. Printing press introduced into Lima.
1580. Buenos Aires re-established.
1591. First newssheet published in Bogotá.
1594. First newssheet published in Lima.
1620–1765. Era of pirates, buccaneers, and freebooters who preyed upon Spanish colonies and trading vessels.
1671. Sir Henry Morgan sacked Panama.
1693. First periodical published in New Spain, *El Mercurio Volante*.
1701. French ships granted right to trade in Spanish American ports.
1718. Viceroyalty of New Granada established.
1767. Jesuits expelled from Spanish American colonies.
1776. Viceroyalty of La Plata created.
1780. Revolt of Tupac Amaru II in Peru.
1781. Revolt of the *comuneros* in New Granada.
—— Conspiracy in Chile.
1787. Printing press introduced into Havana.
1791. *El Mercurio Peruano*, a historical and literary magazine, began publication
1794. Printing press introduced into New Granada.
1796. English seized a portion of Panama.
1797. English conquered Trinidad Island.
—— Revolt in Caracas for independence. Crushed.
1801. *El Telégrafo Mercantil*, periodical, founded in Buenos Aires.
1805. *El Diario de México* began publication.
1806. English captured Buenos Aires. Expelled.
—— Miranda's first attempt at revolution in Venezuela.

1806. Printing press introduced into Venezuela.
1807. English seized Montevideo. Forced to evacuate.
1808. Napoleon invaded Spain and placed his brother Joseph on the Spanish throne.
—— First revolutionary disturbances in Mexico.
1809. *Junta* established in Quito and movement for independence begun.
1810. *Junta* of Caracas established.
—— *Junta* of Buenos Aires established May 25.
—— *Junta* of Chile established.
—— *Junta* of Cartagena in New Granada formed.
—— Beginning of Hidalgo's revolution in Mexico with the *Grito de Dolores*.
1811. Capture and execution of Hidalgo and Allende in Mexico. Morelos assumed leadership of the revolution.
—— Printing press introduced into Chile.
—— Declaration of independence in Venezuela.
—— Declaration of independence in Ecuador.
—— Victory of Manuel Belgrano at Tucumán.
1812. Disastrous earthquake in Venezuela caused defeat of Miranda's attempts at revolution.
1813. Belgrano's army destroyed by royalists.
—— Bolívar won first victories in the north.
1814. Montevideo captured by patriots.
—— Bolívar proclaimed Liberator and made president of Venezuela.
—— San Martín made commander of Argentine army.
1814–1817. San Martín trained an army at Mendoza.
1815. Capture and execution of Morelos. Mexican revolution checked.
1816. Declaration of independence in Argentina.
—— Brazil captured Montevideo.
—— Miranda died in a dungeon in Spain.
1817. San Martín crossed the Andes and defeated the Spanish army at Chacabuco.
—— Bernardo O'Higgins made governor of Chile.
1818. Final defeat of royalists in Chile at Maipú.
1819. Bolívar's army crossed the Andes and won a victory at Boyacá in New Granada.

1819. United States of Colombia established, Bolívar president.
1820. San Martín, aided by Lord Cochrane, landed troops in Peru.
—— Beginning of Iturbide's revolution in Mexico.
1821. Proclamation of the Plan de Iguala.
—— The last viceroy to Mexico, Juan O'Donojú, signed the Treaty of Cordoba in recognition of the independence of Mexico. Iturbide elected ruler.
—— Bolívar's victory at Carabobo in Venezuela established independence in the north.
—— Independence of Peru proclaimed by San Martín.
1822. Ecuador won its independence by the victory of Pichincha and was incorporated into Bolívar's republic of Colombia.
—— Celebrated interview of San Martín and Bolívar in Guayaquil.
—— San Martín resigned his command of the army and left America for France.
—— Iturbide proclaimed emperor of Mexico.
1823. Abdication of Iturbide.
1824. Execution of Iturbide. New constitution promulgated. Guadalupe Victoria elected president.
—— Bolívar's great victory at Junín in Peru, followed by the complete defeat of the Spaniards at Ayacucho. La Serna, last viceroy, surrendered.
1825. Royalists driven from Bolivia.
1826. Last royalist troops driven from Callao.

After Independence

Argentina

1824. Rivadavia elected president.
1825–1827. War with Brazil.
1825–1835. Struggle between Federalists and Unitarians for power.
1835–1852. Dictatorship of Rosas.
1850. San Martín died in France.
1852. Fall of Rosas in the battle of Monte Caseros.
1853. Constitution adopted.
1853–1859. Urquiza's regime.
1859. Buenos Aires joined the confederation of the provinces.

1861. Defeat of Urquiza at Pavón.
1862. Buenos Aires became national capital.
—— Bartolomé Mitre became president and started the progress of the republic.
1865–1867. War with Paraguay.
1868. Sarmiento became the "schoolmaster president."
1869. *La Prensa*, a great newspaper, established.
1870. *La Nación*, another famous newspaper, established.
—— Revolution in Entre Ríos. Urquiza murdered.
1877. Rosas died in England.
1880. Remains of San Martín brought from France to Buenos Aires.
1903. The Christ of the Andes erected.
1912. Electoral reforms, including secret and compulsory voting.
1916. Radical Civic Union came into power. Hipólito Irigoyen became president. He kept Argentina neutral in the World War.
1928. Irigoyen again elected president.
1930. Irigoyen ousted by a comparatively bloodless revolution.
1932. Agustín Justo took office as president.
1933. Hipólito Irigoyen died. His funeral was attended by 250,000 persons.
1934. The thirty-second international Eucharistic Congress convened at Buenos Aires.
1936. Meeting in Buenos Aires of the Inter-American Conference for the Maintenance of Peace.
1938. The new president, Roberto M. Ortiz, a Liberal, outlined an eight-point program for social and economic reforms.

Uruguay

1817. Brazil took Montevideo.
1825. Uruguay declared its independence from Brazil.
1827. Defeat of Brazil at Ituzaingó.
1828. Establishment of the *República Oriental del Uruguay.*
1830. Constitution adopted.
1835–1931. Intermittent struggle between the *Colorados* and the *Blancos.*
1843–1852. Montevideo besieged by Rosas.

1917. Constitutional reforms, including a secret ballot and minority representation.
1928. Law of dual nationality.
1933. Seventh Pan American Congress assembled at Montevideo.
1934. New constitution adopted.

Paraguay

1811. Won independence from Argentina.
—— *Junta* formed.
1813. Constitution adopted.
1814–1840. Dictatorship of Francia.
1844–1870. Dictatorships of the López.
1864–1870. War with Brazil.
1870. Constitution proclaimed.
1876–1923. Intermittent revolutionary upheavals.
1912–1916. President Schaerer served a complete term, the first president since 1870 to do this.
1932–1938. Chaco war with Bolivia.
1938. Air service inaugurated by the Pan American Airways between Rio de Janeiro and Buenos Aires by way of Asunción.

Chile

1822. Bernardo O'Higgins named Supreme Director.
—— The first constitution inaugurated.
1823–1830. Ten governments and three different constitutions.
1827–1829. Five revolutions.
1828. A republican constitution adopted under a liberal president, Francisco Antonio Pinto.
1829. Civil war. Conservatives victorious.
1830–1861. Rule of the conservatives.
1833. A new constitution promulgated.
1836. War with Peru and Bolivia. Chile victorious.
1842. University of Chile founded.
1851. Revolution by the liberals.
1858. Another rebellion of the liberals.
1861–1891. Period of liberal control.
1865–1866. War with Spain.

1869–1871. War with the Araucanian Indians.

1879–1883. War of the Pacific with Peru and Bolivia. Chile the victor.

1886. Balmaceda became president.

1891. Bitter civil war. Conservative victory.

1901. Liberals return to power.

1910. Trans-Andean railroad completed.

1920. Arturo Alessandri, candidate of the Liberal Alliance, elected president.

1925. Reform of the fiscal system and the peso put on a gold basis.

1927. Carlos Ibáñez elected president.

1929. Tacna-Arica dispute settled.

1931. Downfall of Ibáñez.

1932. Alessandri again elected president.

1935. Approval of the Colonization Law governing the ownership of land below the Bío Bío River and on Chiloé Island.

1937–1938. Political agitation led by Nazis and Leftists, whose candidates were defeated in the presidential elections.

1939. Disastrous earthquake ruined 20 cities. Unsuccessful plots to overthrow the government.

Peru

1823. Constitution adopted.

1825. Bolívar dictator.

1826–1879. Civil struggles.

1860. A new constitution.

1879–1883. War of the Pacific. Ended with the Treaty of Ancón. Chile victorious.

1920. A new constitution.

1929. Tacna-Arica dispute with Chile settled.

1930. Eleven-year-old dictatorship of Augusto B. Leguia overthrown. A succession of provisional presidents.

1933. Assassination of President Sánchez Cerro by a member of the Aprista party.

1934. Commemoration of the 400th anniversary of the founding of Cuzco.

1937. Industrial reforms. The first model village opened in Lima for the families of workers.

1938. The Eighth Pan American Conference convened at Lima.

1939. Unsuccessful revolt against President Oscar R. Benavides.

Bolivia

1819–1825. Battleground for independence.

1825. Royalists defeated and Bolivia became independent.

1826. Constitution promulgated. General Sucre first president.

1831,1843, 1851. New constitutions adopted.

1825–1899. Intermittent revolutions and foreign wars. Sixty revolutions in 74 years and six presidents killed.

1861, 1880. New constitutions.

1879–1883. War of the Pacific.

1900. An era of comparative peace began.

1932–1938. Chaco war with Paraguay.

1939. President Germán Busch set up a totalitarian state, dismissing Congress and abolishing all courts. Later the President committed suicide and a provisional president took charge of the government.

Ecuador

1822. Independence won in battle of Pichincha. Ecuador incorporated with Colombia.

1830. Ecuador proclaimed independence from Colombia. Constitution adopted. General Flores first president and real founder of the republic.

1835, 1843. New constitutions.

1830–1916. A series of revolutions, new presidents, and twelve new constitutions.

1859. War with Peru.

1925. Government overthrown by General Gómez.

1931. Revolution ousted President Isidro Ayora.

1935–1937. Dictatorship of Federico Páez.

1937–1939. Political unrest, quick succession of presidents.

Colombia

1822. Republic formed of Colombia, Venezuela, and Ecuador. Bolívar president.

1830. Constitution formulated. Bolívar retired and died at Santa Marta.

1830–1886. New presidents, revolutions, constitutions.

1899–1903. Civil War.

1903. Revolution in Panama resulting in independence.

1914–1930. New presidents and constitutions. Era of peace began.

1934. The disputed Leticia region was taken over by Colombia.

1935. Boundary line settled with Peru.

Venezuela

1830. Venezuela declared independent of Colombia. Constitution adopted. Páez first president.

1835–1910. New presidents, revolts, new constitutions.

1910–1935. Regime of Juan Vicente Gómez.

1925. The fifteenth constitution adopted.

1933. Celebration of the 150th anniversary of Bolívar's birth.

1935. Death of Vicente Gómez, dictator of twenty-five years, and return of many political exiles.

Mexico

1824–1834. Federal Republic.

1828. Revolution.

1829. Attempted abolition of slavery and expulsion of native Spaniards.

1833. Santa Anna declared dictator.

1834–1846. Centralized Republic.

1836. Mexico lost Texas.

1845–1848. War with the United States. Ended by the treaty of Guadalupe-Hidalgo.

1846–1847 Second period of the Federal Republic.

1857–1917. Government under constitution of 1857.

1858. Benito Juárez became president.

1858–1861. War of the Reform.

1862. French invasion.

1864–1867. Reign of Maximilian.

1867–1872. Rule of Juárez.

1877–1880. First presidency of Porfirio Díaz.

1884–1911. Age of Díaz.

1910–1920. Period of anarchy.

1917–1930. Government under new constitution of 1917.

1932. Discovery of the Monte Albán treasures.

1933. Adoption of the Six-Year Plan.

1934. Lázaro Cárdenas inaugurated president.

1936. Expulsion of ex-president Calles. The Laredo-Mexico City highway opened.

1939. A second Six-Year Plan announced.

Cuba

1538. Havana rebuilt by Hernando de Soto.

1628. Havana raided by the Dutch.

1762. Havana captured by the English. Released 1763.

1765. French introduced coffee and bee-culture.

1790. An era of progress began.

1812–1824. Spain's constitution applied to Cuba. Era of prosperity.

1823. A revolutionary movement was crushed.

1824. Governor-general was given complete control over Cuba. Oppression began.

1844. An unsuccessful uprising of negro slaves.

1849–1851. Three unsuccessful attempts at revolt by Narciso López, who was captured and executed.

1868–1878. Revolt and the Republic of Cuba established under Céspedes. Rebellion finally put down.

1879. Right of representation in the Spanish Cortes granted Cuba.

1886. Slavery abolished.

1895–1898. Revolution initiated by Martí.

1898. Spanish American War. Spain renounced her rights over Cuba, Puerto Rico, and other islands of the Antilles. Independent government organized.

1901. Constitution adopted.

1902. Tomás Estrada Palma first president.

1906–1909. Government taken over by the United States. American troops withdrawn 1909.

1917. United States troops landed to restore order.

1920–1921. A severe financial depression.

1924. Machado, a liberal, became president.

1930– . Political unrest.

1931. New Capitol dedicated in Havana. Cuban Central Highway completed across the island.
1933. Flight of President Gerardo Machado and succession of provisional presidents.
1934. Platt Amendment abolished.
1939. Revision of the constitution.
1940. Elections under a new constitution.

INDEX

Numbers refer to pages.